emotional
intelligence

PEARSON

At Pearson, we believe in learning – all kinds of learning for all kinds of people. Whether it's at home, in the classroom or in the workplace, learning is the key to improving our life chances.

That's why we're working with leading authors to bring you the latest thinking and the best practices, so you can get better at the things that are important to you. You can learn on the page or on the move, and with content that's always crafted to help you understand quickly and apply what you've learned.

If you want to upgrade your personal skills or accelerate your career, become a more effective leader or more powerful communicator, discover new opportunities or simply find more inspiration, we can help you make progress in your work and life.

Pearson is the world's leading learning company. Our portfolio includes the Financial Times, Penguin, Dorling Kindersley, and our educational business, Pearson International.

Every day our work helps learning flourish, and wherever learning flourishes, so do people.

To learn more please visit us at: **www.pearson.com/uk**

brilliant

emotional
intelligence

Harness the power of emotions;
succeed in all areas of your life

Gill Hasson

Harlow, England • London • New York • Boston • San Francisco • Toronto • Sydney • Auckland • Singapore • Hong Kong
Tokyo • Seoul • Taipei • New Delhi • Cape Town • São Paulo • Mexico City • Madrid • Amsterdam • Munich • Paris • Milan

PEARSON EDUCATION LIMITED

Edinburgh Gate
Harlow
Essex CM20 2JE
England

and Associated Companies throughout the world

Visit us on the World Wide Web at:
www.pearson.com/uk

First published 2012

© Pearson Education Limited 2012

ISBN: 978-0-273-77657-4

British Library Cataloguing-in-Publication Data
A catalogue record for this book is available from the British Library

Library of Congress Cataloging-in-Publication Data
A catalog record for this book is available from the Library of Congress

10 9 8 7 6 5 4 3 2 1
16 15 14 13 12

Set in Plantin 10/14pt by 30.
Printed in Great Britain by Henry Ling Ltd, at the Dorset Press, Dorchester,
Dorset.

Contents

About the author

Gill Hasson is a tutor and trainer. She currently teaches academic study skills at the University of Sussex and delivers courses and training for youth workers, social workers, foster parents, pre-school workers and adult education tutors. These courses include assertiveness and confidence building, personal development, communication skills, child and adolescent development. She has written courses on the subjects of health and childcare for the Open University. Gill is co-author of *Bounce: Use the power of resilience to live the life you want* (Pearson 2009) and *How to be Assertive* (Pearson 2010). She is also the author of *Brilliant Communication Skills* (Pearson 2011).

Gill lives with her husband, youngest son and Norman the cat in a house at the top of a hill in Brighton. You can contact her at gillhasson@btinternet.com.

Acknowledgements

Thanks again to Roz, Lennie, Colleen and Phil. Also to John MacDonald. And Sue, Janine and Gilly for their continuing interest.

Introduction

> *When dealing with people, remember you are not dealing with creatures of logic, but creatures of emotion.*
>
> Dale Carnegie

Emotions are what drive us and emotions can also lead us astray. In Latin, emotions are described as 'motus anima' meaning 'the spirit that moves us'.

No matter how logical, reasonable and rational we think we are, it is our emotions that motivate and propel us. Emotions play a key part in the way we perceive, understand and reason about people and things.

It's easy to dismiss the mess and muddle of emotions as interference with rational reasoning and decision-making; we tend to see intellect as separate from and superior to emotions. Emotional intelligence, however, recognises that intellect and emotions are mutually inclusive; they are both as important as each other.

intellect and emotions are mutually exclusive; they are both important

Emotional intelligence involves a set of skills that defines how effectively you perceive, understand, use and manage your own and others' feelings. It is the most important factor in how well you get on with others professionally as well as personally.

We probably all know people who are brilliant at identifying and managing emotions; they're able to recognise and understand their feelings as well as being able to express them in an appropriate manner. They don't let emotions overwhelm them in difficult situations; they can manage a range of emotions such as disappointment, jealousy and guilt appropriately.

They are comfortable with who they are. They are not afraid to show appreciation, empathy and compassion for other people. Emotionally intelligent people are in tune with themselves and those around them. They're excellent decision makers, and they know when to trust and use their intuition.

They are also very good communicators; in most circumstances they know what to say, how to say it and, most importantly, when to say it. They delegate wisely and find it relatively easy to persuade and influence other people. They do not though, use manipulation and emotional blackmail to get things done.

They are able to manage anger in appropriate ways and are not afraid to stand up for what they believe. They are not afraid to cry if they are hurt. They are willing to admit that they are wrong, and are not embarrassed to say they are sorry.

Regardless of their strengths, they're usually willing to look at themselves honestly; they take responsibility for their emotions and don't blame others for how they feel. They accept challenges and are able to manage setbacks. They are positive and optimistic about themselves, the others around them and life in general. They know themselves very well, and they're also able to sense and manage the emotional needs of others.

Would you like to be more like this? This book will show you how.

How to use this book

Brilliant Emotional Intelligence has two parts to it. In Part 1 you will learn how to identify, understand and use emotions. Part 2 discusses how to use your emotional intelligence in specific situations.

Of course, I want you to read this book from cover to cover; I want you to start at Chapter 1 and read through to Chapter 15. But I also know that if you're like me, this is the sort of book you might like to dip in and out of. So, if you want to get straight to the point and learn how to manage your emotions, turn to Chapter 6. To learn how to manage other people's feelings and emotions, go straight to Chapter 7.

However, if you would like to start with a better understanding of the existence and nature of emotions, start with Chapter 1 and then read Chapter 4.

Want to know how emotionally intelligent you are? Then turn straight to the quiz in Chapter 2. It will help to highlight your strengths. It will also identify areas and situations where you could develop your emotional intelligence. Whatever your levels of emotional intelligence though, if you'd like to know more about why you and other people respond in the ways that we do, turn to Chapter 3.

Research shows that for all of us, a whopping 93 per cent of emotions and feelings are communicated nonverbally. So, if you want to develop your emotional intelligence, it makes sense to be more aware of nonverbal behaviour. Chapter 5 will help.

Throughout Part 1 I have included plenty of practical ideas and techniques to help you put theory into practice. You will pick up tips on such things as, for example, how to change the way you think about emotions, how to tune in to your intuition, how to help children to develop their emotional intelligence

> 93 per cent of emotions and feelings are communicated nonverbally

and how other people can help you develop *your* emotional intelligence. Follow the tips and techniques that appeal to you most and you will soon improve your emotional intelligence in notable ways.

However, navigating your way through specific situations often requires specific advice. Part 2 looks at some particular situations such as delegating, persuading and influencing others. For advice on what to do when you are disappointed or feel guilty, turn to Chapters 10 and 14.

If you want to know what underlies anger and how to manage both your own and other people's anger, Chapter 12 will help you.

Finally, there's good news and there's bad news. Apart from *receiving* bad news, one of the toughest emotional challenges is to *deliver* bad news. Turn to Chapter 15 to learn how to do this firmly and tactfully.

The good news is that, unlike delivering bad news, when it comes to giving praise and compliments, you don't have to worry about getting the wording exactly right; a genuine sentiment phrased a bit awkwardly is better than no appreciation being showed at all. Read Chapter 13 to discover how to use your emotional intelligence to make a positive difference. That's emotionally intelligent!

And, the more emotional intelligence you have, the more likely you are to handle the good times and the bad times in life, to understand and manage your own emotions and other people's, to form strong, productive relationships that make things happen and to succeed both personally and professionally.

Brilliant!

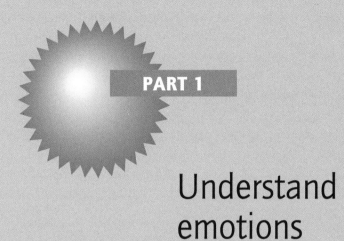

PART 1

Understand emotions

CHAPTER 1

Emotions and emotional intelligence

On the first evening of their holiday in Rome, Jo and Alex left their hotel to go out for dinner. They were waiting on the pavement for the light to change so that they could cross the street, when a man came up behind Alex. Jo froze as the man put his arm round Alex's neck and with his other hand, pinned Alex's arms to his sides. Quick as a flash, a young woman ran up, snatched Jo's bag and, despite Alex's struggle to free himself, grabbed Alex's wallet from his pocket. The pair ran off and although Alex chased after them, the man and woman disappeared down a narrow side street.

Neither Alex nor Jo were hurt but Jo was terrified; her heart started pounding, she felt weak and shaky and started to cry. All colour had drained from Alex – his face was white.

They made their way back down the same street to their hotel – looking around them all the time. Jo was still shaking when they walked back into the hotel lobby. The man on reception was horrified when Jo and Alex told him what had happened; he brought them a drink and then called the police.

While they waited for the police to arrive Jo started shivering and felt sick. The police arrived and took Jo and Alex to the central Rome police station to file a report.

Returning to their hotel the shaky feeling was starting to wear off and instead, Jo started to feel angry that they had been targeted in this way. Alex felt unable to think or say much and he remained very quiet.

Once back in their room, Alex dropped onto the bed with relief and fell asleep. However Jo couldn't sleep: she stayed awake most of the night going over in her mind what had happened.

Although neither Jo nor Alex was physically hurt, their minds and bodies were experiencing a strong emotional reaction to a dramatic situation.

What are emotions?

Emotions bridge thought, feeling, and action – they affect many aspects of a person, and the person affects many aspects of the emotions.

John D. Mayer in a 2000 interview with Josh Freedman.
See: http://www.6seconds.org/2000/06/25/what-are-emotions/

We may not all have experienced a mugging, but like Jo and Alex, most of us have experienced fear and anger. Along with surprise, joy, sadness and disgust they are generally acknowledged as the six basic universal emotions; experienced by everyone no matter what their age, gender, experience or culture.

That doesn't mean that emotions are simple. Why? Because there is more than one aspect to an emotion.

Everyone knows what an emotion is until asked to give a definition. Then it seems, nobody knows.

B. Fehr and J. Russell

It's probably easiest to define emotions as feelings but feelings are just one part of a process that involves thoughts, behaviour and feedback loops. Emotions have both physical and mental aspects which *interact* with each other.

Physical aspect

This part of an emotion is the physical changes that occur in your body when you experience an emotion.

For both Jo and Alex, this included an increased heart rate, sweating, crying and the release of adrenaline in response to what happened.

Although people might have different *cognitive* responses to the same situation – that is, their thoughts might differ – people have very similar *physical* responses to the same emotion. Regardless of age, race, or gender, when, for example, we are experiencing stress, our bodies release adrenaline; this hormone helps prepare the body to either run away or fight; the 'fight or flight' reaction.

Furthermore, more than one emotion can produce the same physical reaction. Fear, anger and excitement, for example, can *all* be characterised by increased heart rate, rapid breathing and the release of adrenaline.

Behavioural aspect

This aspect of an emotion is the outward expression of emotion; the things you do, your actions (or inaction) when you experience an emotion.

How a person behaves when they experience an emotion depends on a number of variables, including each person's ability to manage the situation and how the situation relates to the person's past experiences. For example, when they were attacked, Jo froze. Alex, on the other hand attempted to fight off and chase the assailants.

The outward expression of an emotion also gives other people clues to someone's emotional state and helps to guide their response; Jo and Alex's distressed behaviour triggered concern and consideration in the hotel receptionist.

outward expressions of emotions mean different things in different cultures

Outward expressions of emotions mean different things in different cultures. For example, in some cultures, if a person avoids eye contact it is taken as a sign of respect. In other cultures, in certain contexts, lack of eye contact might suggest guilt.

Cognitive aspect

This aspect of an emotion involves what you think; your perception and interpretation when something happens. The cognitive aspect is the internal 'feeling' part of an emotion – the conscious, subjective element of an emotion.

Subjective feelings cannot be easily observed or measured; instead, the person experiencing the emotion must describe it to others, and each person's interpretation and description of a feeling may be slightly different.

So, although Jo and Alex experienced the same event, they will not experience or describe their feelings in exactly the same ways.

brilliant example

On the day that Clare married Josh, she felt elated. Josh was an attractive young man with a good job. He was kind and thoughtful. However, Josh had a drink problem. At the same time that Clare was feeling elated, Josh felt proud, Clare's sister felt sad, Clare's parents felt concern, and Josh's parents felt relief. Each person's thoughts about the same situation triggered a different emotion. (Although each of them had a similar physical response; tears!)

Whether you are aware of it or not, when you experience any emotion, it is made up of these three elements; physical, behavioural and cognitive.

Below are three situations. Each situation has provoked an emotion and each emotion has a physical response and possible cognitive and behavioural responses.

Situation: Being mugged
Emotion: Fear

- **Physical response:** racing heart, rapid breathing.
- **Cognitive response:** 'I am in danger.' 'I'm going to get hurt.' 'They won't get away with this.' 'Oh my God. Oh my God. Oh my God.'
- **Behavioural:** freeze, run, attack, cry.

Situation: Passing your driving test
Emotion: Joy

- **Physical response:** increased heartbeat and breathing rate.
- **Cognitive response:** 'Yes! I can't wait to tell everyone.' 'I can't believe I've passed.'
- **Behavioural response:** punching the air, phoning and texting friends and family to share the good news.

Situation: Your team loses in the cup final
Emotion: Sadness

- **Physical response:** deep, slow breathing.
- **Cognitive response:** 'It's not fair. We deserved to win.' 'Oh well, there's always next year.'
- **Behavioural response:** inaction. Drowning your sorrows.

There is no one specific order in which the aspects of an emotion occur, but any one aspect can affect the others. For example, what you think can affect how you feel physically. It can also alter how you behave. Equally, what you do – how you behave – can affect how you feel and what you think. In Chapter 5 for example, you will discover that recent research confirms that what you do – how you sit or stand – can affect how you physically feel and what you think.

brilliant tip

Next time you experience an emotion – for example anger, joy, guilt, pride – try to identify all the different parts of it. Breaking an emotion down into smaller parts makes it easier to see how the different parts are connected, how they interact and how they affect a person.

Emotions and moods

Emotions are related to, but different from, mood. Emotions such as fear and surprise, for example, are specific reactions to a particular event that are usually temporary and last a relatively short time.

On the other hand, moods are longer lasting but less specific, less intense, and not so likely to be triggered by a particular occurrence or event. Moods are a more general feeling such as gloom, misery, apathy, contentment or cheerfulness that last for a longer time; hours or days.

Emotions are more short lived and have a clear object or cause; they are directed at or are about something. You may feel irritated by something specific – someone biting their nails. But a mood can make it more likely that you will feel an emotion. For example, you may be in an irritable mood – where you are easily irritated by someone biting their nails.

Where do your emotions come from?

Your emotions come from your limbic brain – the area of your brain that reacts to the world around you instinctively without rational thought or reasoning. In fact limbic (emotional) responses are hard wired into your system, which makes them difficult to hide. (Just try suppressing a startled response when something makes you jump.)

You use the limbic part of your brain when you react to other people and events with your emotions. So, limbic responses are a genuine reflection of your feelings, attitudes and intentions.

Another area of your brain the neo cortex – the new brain – is responsible for your cognitive abilities; thinking, remembering and reasoning. You use the neo cortex part of your brain to formulate, control and verbally express your thoughts, ideas and opinions.

Why do you have emotions?

All emotions have a positive intent that serve physical, personal and social purposes.

Physical safety

Firstly, emotions protect you. They keep you safe. Emotions are used as shortcuts to process information and influence behaviour. They get you to react quickly in circumstances where rational thinking is too slow; for example, in a potentially dangerous situation, you need to react quickly and emotions, like fear and surprise, help you do just that.

These instant responses that compel you to act are limbic driven surges from the viscera – the large internal organs, especially those in the abdomen. They can be seen as *'gut instinct'* or *intuition.*

Your intellect may be confused, but your emotions will never lie to you.

Roger Ebert

These responses are not moderated by conscious thought; by rationalising or reasoning. Instead, they are instant – an emotional reaction to something, and often one of unease and alarm, warning you of danger and getting you to move out of harm's way. These limbic surges can, though, also alert you to a golden opportunity!

brilliant example

Lauren was driving her family to visit friends in London when she became aware of the smell of petrol fumes. Suddenly gripped with fear, she pulled over and insisted her husband and three children get out the car immediately. They called a breakdown service and when he arrived, the mechanic told them that the fuel pipe had come apart. 'One spark and you'd all have gone up in smoke', he said. Gut feeling, instinct, intuition or sixth sense. Whatever you want to call it, Lauren was overtaken by an internal state that compelled her to focus, pay attention and take action.

Tune in to your intuition

When something feels uncomfortable or just not right, acting on your intuition can keep you safe. Here's how to tune in to your intuition and recognise when it's warning you.

Listen to your body

When something doesn't feel right, or you feel unsure about something, the physical aspect of an emotion will often guide you.

the physical aspect of an emotion will often guide you

For example, how do you feel when you have agreed to do something that you really do not want to do? Do you feel queasy? Tense? Your body gives you information that you may not take much notice of but if you ignore those messages, you lose out on valuable information that can let you know what is good for you and what isn't.

Start being more aware of your physical feelings in everyday situations so that you know when your body is warning you.

Pay attention to the feelings, images and words that come to your mind
Feelings of unease or discomfort may be signals alerting you to potential misfortune prompting you to respond. Your inner voice telling you 'this isn't right' and mental images of trouble and misfortune also play a part in the way your intuition speaks to you.

Becoming more conscious of your emotions and feelings on an everyday basis will serve you well when the bigger, more important messages need to get through, so pay attention!

Ignore distractions
Focus. Once you become aware of your unease, don't allow anything else to divert your attention. Listening to intuition is like tuning in to a radio station. You can't hear several stations all at once, you just need to hear one station clearly.

Things don't add up
Your mind and body are constantly picking up information from the world around you, even when you're not really conscious of it. Anything that you are aware of as being out of place or unusual means your intuition is warning you.

Of course, the reverse is also true – when all the information your senses are receiving does add up, your intuition is giving you positive messages!

The next time you need to make a decision, tune into your intuition. Don't get neurotic about it, just be more aware of what happens when you tune into and follow your intuition.

And, when you notice what your intuition is telling you but *don't* act on it, what's the outcome?

Fear is an example of an emotion that has a very clear purpose; to protect you. It is thought that fear is just one of the six basic emotions that we all have. The other basic emotions – surprise, sadness, disgust, anger and joy – also have clear purposes that help us to manage and survive.

- Surprise allows you to respond to a sudden unexpected event.
- Sadness helps you to adjust to a loss of some kind.
- Disgust warns you to withdraw from something or someone.
- Anger leads to you retaliating in response to being wronged.
- Joy allows you to value and appreciate something or someone.

Emotions don't just help each of us to survive though. There are other reasons for emotions; emotions have social value.

Social value of emotions

We would not be able to maintain and develop relationships and communities so well if we did not, for example, have a sense of guilt, shame, embarrassment and pride.

These are the emotions that we experience as a result of our ability to reflect on and adapt the way we behave and relate to others. Trust, for example, leads to sharing and cooperating. Guilt motivates you to put right something you should or shouldn't have done and seek forgiveness.

When you experience a social emotion, you are aware that your actions and behaviour have been or will be perceived, judged by and affect others.

For example, imagine you were introduced to someone, 'This is Jane', and your reply was 'How nice to meet you – Natalie has told me a lot about her Mum', and Jane replied 'I'm not

Natalie's Mum, I'm her sister'. The embarrassment and shame that arise will probably cause you to blush, apologise and reflect that in future you will not make assumptions like that! To your relief the embarrassment that Jane feels prompts her to minimise the issue for you, her and Natalie by laughing and insisting she's not upset.

The situation with you, Jane and Natalie illustrates how coordinated human emotions can be; an emotion in one person (embarrassment) can trigger another emotion (forgiveness) in the other person, which keeps everyone in balance and safeguards the whole group.

Social emotions enable you to feel emotionally connected and attached to others; to feel that you are accepted, included and that you belong. To feel that you are understood, valued and respected. To feel that you are liked, loved, admired, appreciated, approved of, cared for and needed. To feel trusted, supported and, when appropriate, forgiven.

Finally, social emotions enable you to reciprocate those feelings; to understand, empathise, like, love, support, have concern and care for other people.

Creativity and self-actualisation

As well as providing safety and social value, emotions serve our creative needs. Emotions can enhance, magnify, broaden or narrow experience; provide depth, focus and differentiation.

For many of us, there is a close link between emotional experience and creativity. Art, music and literature all deal on a fundamental level with provoking and inspiring emotions and creating an emotional connection between the art, music, literature etc. and the viewer, listener or reader. Think, for example, of the way music is used in films to help provoke and/or emphasise sadness, fear, joy and triumph.

As well as being able to appreciate creative output, there is also a close link between emotional experience and our ability to be creative. Research has found that how a person is feeling affects this ability.

According to research at the University of Toronto, positive, happy emotions and moods may open your mind and increase your creative thinking.[1]

In the study, volunteers were asked to solve two types of problems – a creative problem requiring word associations or a visual problem that required ignoring distracting information. First though, participants listened to either happy or sad music, and were asked to think about happy or sad things.

The 'happy' participants were able to perform well on creative problem-solving tasks. However, happy participants also tended to be more distracted, and, as a result, didn't do well on visual tasks with distracting information. Conversely, those participants who were in a sad mood, did well on the visual tasks – they were able to focus and concentrate. They performed poorly on creative problem-solving tasks.

Why was this? It would appear that the part of the brain called the amygdala could have quite an impact on your creativity.

The amygdala triggers fear and anxiety. Fear enables you to focus your attention on potential threats; everything else falls out of this focus and doesn't matter. So you shut out superfluous information and shut down the part of the brain that makes you creative.

Of course, this can be very helpful in some situations. If, for example, you are asked to give a presentation at a conference about your department's achievements, your anxiety and nerves will prompt you to focus and prepare well.

On the other hand, positive emotions tend to spur creativity; when you are happy, the amygdala is quiet so that you can open up your perspective and broaden your world. This allows you to indulge your imagination – to see new ideas and try new things, explore, learn new information, make links, connections and comparisons.

But what about, you might ask, all those tortured artists, whose pain is the source of their creativity? It would appear that rather than be open to and inspired by a range of possibilities, relationships and ideas, they are inspired by how they *feel* – they are expressing their *feelings* in their art.

Emotions then, serve your creative needs. Emotions can broaden or narrow experience; provide depth and focus. Emotions can help provide a sense of meaning, purpose and achievement. Emotions allow you to feel competent and capable to have a sense of autonomy and control; to be able to make and implement choices.

Finally, emotions give you feelings of self-respect and self-esteem. And, as we've just seen, if you feel good

> if you feel good about yourself you have the confidence to broaden your experiences

about yourself you have the confidence to broaden your experiences; to reach out and connect with and make a contribution to the world. To realise your potential!

Is it possible to 'lose' your emotions?

Twenty-five year old Phineas Gage was a railroad worker in Vermont, USA. On September 13, 1848, an explosion blew a thin iron rod – one metre long and three centimetres in diameter-through Gage's left cheek. It ripped into his brain and exited through his skull, landing 20 metres away.

Incredibly, he survived. He was conscious, able to talk and walk immediately afterwards. But it seems he changed overnight, from a

▶

responsible, sociable, capable man into an impatient, impulsive and indecisive one.

John Martyn Harlow, the doctor who treated him for a few months afterward, wrote that Gage's friends found him 'no longer Gage'. The balance between his 'intellectual faculties and animal propensities' seemed to have gone. He was unreliable, uttered 'the grossest profanity' and showed 'little deference for his fellows'.

The iron rod had destroyed most of the front of the left part of his brain. Gage's was one of the first cases to reveal that some faculties can be associated with specific regions of the brain; the frontal lobes.

Today, people with the same area of brain damage appear to be affected in the same way. Often it is found that they have lost not only their ability to reason and rationalise but also their emotions. This shows how closely the two areas are linked and how important emotions are to our powers of reasoning.

What is emotional intelligence?

So far in this chapter, you have learnt that emotions have physical, behavioural and cognitive aspects that interact with each other. You've also seen that emotions have a number of purposes; to protect you, to help you make decisions, to develop and maintain social bonds, to experience creative processes and to realise your potential.

Emotions come from the limbic area of the brain whereas what makes for intelligence – thoughts, reasoning and rationalising comes from the neo cortex.

What though, is intelligence? Intelligence is the ability to learn, to understand and think things out quickly and efficiently; to take in new information, assimilate it and apply it appropriately and effectively.

The meaning of emotional intelligence then, has something to do with the links between emotions and thoughts; between thinking, feeling and doing.

It is very important to understand that emotional intelligence is not the opposite of intelligence, it is not the triumph of head over heart – it is the unique intersection of both.

David Caruso

Emotional intelligence can be seen as having two key principles.

First, emotional intelligence is about being *aware* of emotions – *identifying and understanding* emotions – both your own and other people's emotions.

Second, emotional intelligence is about *using and managing* emotions. Again, your own and other people's.

Lets look at this more closely.

Identifying emotions

At its most simple, identifying an emotion means being able to name or describe an emotion. But it also involves recognising the physical states, the thoughts and actions that make up an emotion. It includes recognising emotions in nonverbal communication and behaviour; in facial expressions, tone of voice and body language for example.

Identifying emotions also involves recognising how clear, typical, influential or reasonable a particular emotion is in a particular context and being able to recognise appropriate and inappropriate expression of emotion.

Understanding emotions

This means making sense and meaning about emotions. Understanding emotions involves knowing that any one aspect (physical, cognitive or behavioural) of an emotion can affect another.

Understanding emotions involves being aware of the differences, transition, variations and degrees of intensity between emotions. Understanding, for example, the difference between anger and frustration, disappointment and regret.

This aspect of emotional intelligence involves an ability to understand how and why you and other people experience certain emotions in certain situations and how emotions impact on social dynamics. Finally, understanding emotions includes knowing when and how emotive language and behaviour is being used.

Using emotions

Using your emotions involves the ability to draw on emotions to help and inform your thinking, reasoning and problem solving. It means using your intuition; using emotions to help make decisions about what to do and not to do – to prioritise thinking and behaviour. It includes knowing how to use emotions to build empathy and rapport with others.

Using emotions also includes knowing how to draw on emotions to create specific moods, such as when happy emotions facilitate inductive reasoning and creativity and inspire and motivate. And, knowing when sad emotions can be induced, for example with the use of sad music at a funeral.

Managing emotions

This involves the ability to manage your own and other people's emotions, according to specific goals and whatever is deemed appropriate in the circumstances, a particular situation or context. Unlike *controlling emotions*, this does not mean dominating or suppressing emotions. *Managing* emotions involves handling emotions with a degree of skill and flexibility.

Managing emotions requires an ability to stay open to feelings, both those that are pleasant and those that are unpleasant. It involves knowing when and how to express emotions and when to rein them in; when to engage or detach from an emotion.

managing emotions involves handling emotions with a degree of skill and flexibility

Emotional intelligence – identifying and understanding, using and managing emotions – is a dynamic process; each ability influencing the other.

Self-awareness   ↔ Other people awareness

↕   ↕

Self-management ↔ Other people management

Following the diagram above, think through an emotional situation – perhaps using an awkward or difficult personal experience you can recall which you either managed well or not so well. For example, imagine a friend phoned you – upset at something you said to her last time you met – she feels you were critical and harsh. Your awareness and understanding of her feelings would impact on your awareness and understanding of your own feelings and vice versa. And, your self-awareness and other person awareness would influence how you managed your emotions and the emotions of the other person.

brilliant recap

- Emotions have both physical and mental aspects which *interact* with each other.
- Emotions come from the limbic area of our brain. Thoughts come from the neo cortex part of our brain.

▶

- Emotions are different from moods. Emotions are more short lived and have a clear cause; they are directed at or are about something. Moods are longer lasting but less specific and less intense.

- All emotions have a positive intent that serve physical, personal and social purposes.

- Emotional intelligence – identifying and understanding, using and managing emotions – is a dynamic process; each ability influences and interacts with the other.

The Library@Riverside
01709 336774
www.rotherham.gov.uk/libraries

Customer ID: ****16107

Title: Brilliant emotional intelligence
ID: 530264378T
Due: 17/Mar/2020 23:59

Total items: 1
25/Feb/2020 16:49

Did you know that your Library Account
also gives you access to thousands of
eBooks, eAudioBooks & eMagazines?

Visit www.rotherham.gov.uk/libraries

Follow us on Facebook & Twitter
@RothLibraries

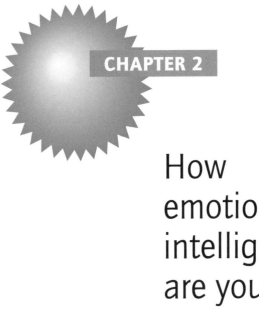

CHAPTER 2

How emotionally intelligent are you?

How emotionally intelligent are you? It's not easy to know. The quiz in this chapter will help. It's *not* a test; the aim is *not* to measure your emotional intelligence – how much emotional intelligence you do or don't have – it's simply to get you thinking about emotions and emotional situations.

Of course you might be tempted to rate yourself with a positive bias. But be honest – being genuine is one of the principles of emotional intelligence; it's not very helpful to start by stretching the truth!

> being genuine is one of the principles of emotional intelligence

On the left hand column are a variety of situations. In the right hand column you rate each situation with marks out of 10.

For example, when you receive an email that leaves you feeling angry, because you find it very difficult to postpone your reply until you calm down, you might rate it with a 2. On the other hand, if a sad film makes you cry and you're not embarrassed and don't try to hide your tears, you would probably rate that situation with a 9 or 10.

Self awareness – identifying and understanding your own emotions	Marks out of 10 (where 10 is easy and 1 is impossible)
If I failed to get a job I'd been interviewed for or a good grade in an exam – if asked, I can admit that I'm disappointed.	
I am aware of how I usually respond when someone criticises me. I know for example, that I either retaliate, reject the criticism, agree or feel crushed.	
If I was half way through a very tedious novel or I signed up for some fitness classes which I wasn't enjoying, I would not continue.	
I'm aware of the difference between feeling angry and frustrated, disappointed or regretful.	
If a friend gets a promotion or a lovely new home or has a fabulous holiday and I wish I could do the same, I can admit that I am jealous.	
In an interview, if asked to describe my strengths, I can identify a couple and give examples of how and when I've used those strengths.	
Total Score	

Managing your emotions	
If someone humiliated me in front of a group of other people I would be able to respond honestly about how I felt and say 'I feel embarrassed and a bit hurt by what you have said.'	
If I receive an email that leaves me feeling angry, I postpone my reply until I calm down.	

At a business meeting or a get together of a mutual friend, I can be civil and polite to a person whom I really dislike.	
If I was anxious about giving a presentation to a group or speaking in public, I would focus my energies and prepare well.	
If a sad film makes me cry, I'm not embarrassed; I don't try to hide my tears.	
If I'm paid a compliment, I can simply reply by saying for example, 'Thanks. That was nice of you to tell me.'	
Total score	

Identifying and understanding other people's emotions

In my group of friends, I am generally aware of how each person feels about others in our social circle.	
If I'm not sure how someone is really feeling I look to see if their body language appears to match what they are saying.	
If I wanted my partner to clean the bathroom I'd wait for a good time to ask him or her; a time he or she would be most likely to agree.	
If a colleague appeared to be avoiding me, I would ask her if she is upset or angry with me.	
I know which people in my life are often negative and get me down and I know which people are usually positive and make me feel good.	
I can usually tell if someone isn't listening.	
Total score	

Managing other people	
If I have to give someone bad news, I know what to say and I am prepared for their response.	
If a friend confided that he prefers one of his children to the other and feels guilty about it, I could reassure him that it's not a dreadful thing to admit.	
At a party, if I noticed another guest had a label hanging out of the back of their collar, I could tell them. (Then move on to a different subject.)	
If I want to show appreciation for something someone has done, I don't let worrying about getting the wording just right stop me from expressing my gratitude.	
In a restaurant, if children are running around, shouting loudly and bashing into my chair, I'd calmly ask the manager to deal with the situation.	
If I had to tell a colleague that he has a BO (body odour) problem, I would find the right words to say and talk to him about it.	
Total Score	

What Does Your Score Mean?

The statements in this quiz focused on four areas of emotional intelligence:

- Self-awareness – identifying and understanding your own emotions.
- Managing your emotions.
- Other people awareness – identifying and managing other peoples emotions.
- Managing other people's emotions.

For any of the four areas that you scored less than 30, it would seem that you don't find it easy to understand or manage emotions and emotional situations in that area. If you scored over 30 in any one area of emotional intelligence, you're doing quite well and for any of the four areas that you scored over 50, you are doing very well!

Go back and read over any area in which you had a high score. It's important to be aware of your strong points and find ways to continue to develop and apply your skills. There are plenty of tips and ideas to help you build on your current strengths and become even more emotionally intelligent. So keep reading!

If, though, you didn't score so well in your responses to identifying and understanding emotions – yours or other people's – you'll find Chapters 4 and 5 particularly helpful. If you didn't score very highly in your responses to managing emotions – both yours and other people's – and would like to improve, Chapters 6 and 7 explain how.

However high your score in any one of the four areas of emotional intelligence, sometimes, in specific situations and with some people, you may feel quite capable. But in other circumstances you may find it difficult to identify, understand or manage emotions.

Like most people you probably have at least one or two situations in each area in which you could be more confident and effective.

Part 2 focuses on specific emotional situations. So, if, for example, you don't find it easy to give bad news, Chapter 15 will guide you through the process. If you struggle to cope when someone makes an unkind comment about you; if you don't find it easy to be civil to someone you dislike, Chapter 11 will give you all the advice you need to manage both yourself and the other person!

Let specific situations or areas where you have a low score guide your development and be an indication of your *eventual* capacity for emotional intelligence.

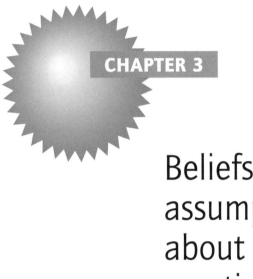

CHAPTER 3

Beliefs and assumptions about emotions

Recently, at a family party, a few of us were talking about plays and films we'd seen and Elaine remarked 'I cry buckets at sad films. It's awful. I don't know what's wrong with me.'

Why did she think that? Where did Elaine learn that it was 'awful' to cry at sad films and that there's 'something wrong' with her?

Our ideas and beliefs about emotions are established quite early in life. Typically, as children, we tend to have intense emotional responses to situations and events – they are often out of proportion to whatever triggered the emotion. We depend on others – parents, family members, teachers – to help us learn to manage what we are feeling.

Although adults sometimes rush to 'fix' or resolve the problem for the child, more often than not, they struggle to actually know how to help the child manage their feelings. Quite simply, they lack emotional intelligence.

Many of us have got the message that certain emotions are 'bad' or 'wrong': we've grown up learning that emotional expression has a variety of negative associations.

Maybe you were reprimanded, even punished for showing emotions. You may, for example, have been punished for expressing anger and frustration when you were small. Or you may have been frightened by the strength of your own bad temper.

Perhaps instead of being allowed to experience and express your feelings, your emotions were often ignored by others, laughed at, invalidated or denied. For example, saying 'I hate my teacher' was met with 'Don't be silly, of course you don't. Get your shoes on and go to school.' Or 'I'm tired' was answered with 'No you're not. Run along and play.'

These sorts of responses might have distracted or pacified you for a while but it did little to teach you about managing feelings and emotions.

Instead, what these responses do is establish beliefs, assumptions and expectations about emotions; that certain emotions are 'bad' or 'wrong'. So, if you're like Elaine, even crying at a sad film will seem wrong.

On the other hand, some of us were brought up in families where an open expression of emotions was normal, with hugs and kisses alternating between tears and angry shouting. In theses families, people laugh and cry and are not afraid to show their anger, fear, frustration and other feelings.

This can cause problems when people from different backgrounds come together. One person may think another over expresses their emotions. Conversely, people who have grown up freely expressing their emotions and feelings might consider the more restrained individuals as being repressed and uptight!

brilliant tip

It's in children that we can see how natural emotions are. Watch how children get angry and sad, happy and excited with spontaneous ease. Notice how the adults around them deal with the child's emotions.

We are all likely to have some unhelpful beliefs about emotions. Fortunately, you can do a number of things to reduce the power of your unhelpful beliefs. One of the most important steps is to increase your awareness of them.

Which of these statements about emotions do you agree with?

- Women shouldn't cry at work. Others might see it as manipulative.
- Never admit to being jealous – you'll lose credibility and the respect of others.
- Pride before a fall; if you are too pleased about something you've achieved, something bad will happen to trip you up.
- If you meet someone who's recently been bereaved, you should avoid talking about the person who's died.
- If someone treats you unfairly, it's wrong to hope that something bad will happen to them. It's also wrong to be pleased when something bad *does* happen to them.
- It's embarrassing to see grown men cry.

One way or another, all these beliefs convey the idea that it's wrong to experience, express or provoke feelings and emotions. So, instead of managing them in an appropriate way we often deal with emotions in inappropriate, unhelpful ways.

Here are some of the unhelpful ways you might deal with emotions:

- Cut yourself off from others or cut other people out.
- Talk about issues and facts rather than opinions and feelings.
- Keep conversations superficial, to avoid getting deep.
- Pretend something hasn't happened or laugh it off – to avoid admitting jealousy, for example.
- Overeat, reach for a drink or drugs.

- Work excessively.

- Exercise compulsively.

The problem is, that if you believe a particular emotion is 'wrong' in some way and you try to ignore or deny an emotion (yours or someone else's) you cut off the opportunity to understand what the emotion is trying to tell you.

But, by their very nature, buried emotions want to surface so you *can* become aware of them, feel them, act on them and release them. Denying, repressing and burying feelings does not get rid of them. Instead, when an emotion is buried, it leaks out in other ways.

when an emotion is buried, it leaks out in other ways

Passive aggressive behaviour is a clear example of leaked feelings. It is an indirect and dishonest expression of feelings and emotions. It involves an avoidance pattern of behaviour; avoiding saying what you feel and what you do and don't want, probably because you've learnt that a direct expression of how you feel is 'wrong'.

Passive aggressive behaviour uses sarcasm, moaning, sulking and other underhand methods to avoid confrontation or avoid saying what you really feel. Anger and frustration are usually suppressed but can be expressed in other, nonverbal ways, for example, giving others 'the silent treatment' or 'dirty looks' when you are unhappy with them. This does not though, let others know what you are really feeling.

When you are behaving in a passive aggressive way, you are reluctant to assert yourself and say what you want and how you feel. Instead, you allow others to take charge, and then you resort to underhand ways, such as manipulation and sabotage, in order to get what you do or do not want. You probably do not even realise you are behaving in such a manipulative way!

On the other hand, if the emotion doesn't 'leak' out, it sits there, building up to an accumulation of repressed feelings. In time, these emotions become distorted: sadness can lead to depression and anger can turn into hatred or resentment, eventually exploding into fits of rage and even violence.

Most of us can think of a time when we've experienced ourselves or someone else suddenly explode in anger at something that seems relatively trivial and harmless; a sure sign that he or she has been trying to control or repress their emotions but the lid has finally blown off!

Change your thinking

Your ability to develop your emotional intelligence largely depends on your willingness to examine and be more flexible about your beliefs, expectations and assumptions about emotions.

↗ exercise 1 Write a 'thinking diary'

How do your beliefs about emotions serve you? Are they helpful or do they lead to unhelpful, negative behaviour?

It is so easy to fall into the trap of negative thinking about emotions. More often than not, you will not even notice you are doing it. One way to become aware of your thoughts is to write them down.

Reflect on what you think about situations and how your thoughts about your feelings make you feel and behave. The more you are aware, the more likely you will be to change unhelpful beliefs.

It's important that you don't just identify emotions such as frustration, disappointment and guilt. Identify emotions that make you feel good; emotions such as being happy, trusting and forgiving. This provides a realistic picture. If you record only negative emotions, your image of yourself will be quite distorted and unrealistic.

▶

Writing it all down might seem a bit taxing, but the process of writing makes the exercise more effective. This is because you have to think twice: before you write and while you are writing.

brilliant example

Sam kept a thinking diary for a week. 'I wrote down several events that happened. They included;

- failing to go to the gym for the third time this week;
- watching my five year old daughter in her school play;
- being congratulated by my manager on a contract I'd secured;
- discovering my home insurance policy didn't cover me for accidental damage;
- having to tell an employee she'd failed an exam.

Obviously I was angry that the insurance policy didn't provide accidental damage cover. What I didn't realise though, was that I sometimes avoid my feelings. For example, when my colleague Nathan, congratulated me on the success of a project I'd worked on, because I felt a bit embarrassed and didn't want to appear conceited I found myself dismissing his compliment, saying 'It was nothing.'

At my daughter's school play, I struggled to maintain my composure in case other parents saw me with a tear in my eye.

I also discovered that I have emotions about emotions! I felt anxious about coping with Gail's reaction when I told her she'd failed her exam. However instead of allowing the guilt I felt as a result of not going to the gym again make me feel bad, it made me realise it was time to cut my losses and cancel my membership. A positive move, I think!

Keeping track of my thoughts helped me to be more aware of what I think about how I feel'

Even though your beliefs and attitudes about emotions may be rooted in childhood, your beliefs *can* be changed; you *can* learn to think in a more positive, helpful way. But just

> you can learn to think in a more positive, helpful way

how do you replace unhelpful and disempowering beliefs about emotions with more useful and empowering ones? There are techniques for challenging unhelpful beliefs.

Look at the thinking diary you have kept. Highlight all the negative thinking and then write out alternative, more positive ways of thinking. As an example, the table below shows how Sam could change his negative, unhelpful ways of thinking to positive, helpful thoughts.

Situation	Negative, unhelpful thought	Positive, helpful thought
Watching my five year old daughter in her school play.	I'm going to cry. I must not let myself cry.	I feel proud. This is an emotional moment. It's fine to shed a few tears.
Being congratulated by my colleague on a contract I'd secured.	Everyone else in the office heard what Nathan said – I'm embarrassed. Best to be modest and dismiss it.	That's nice of him to take the trouble to say that.
Discovering my home insurance policy didn't cover me for accidental damage.	I'm furious! Why didn't they tell me when I bought the policy?	I'm furious! I'd better change the policy and check other insurance policies provide the cover I need. I might also change to a different insurance provider.
Having to tell an employee she'd failed an exam.	Gail is bound to start crying. I'll feel uncomfortable and will try to get her to stop.	Gail might cry when I tell her. That's understandable – she'll be upset that after all that studying she didn't pass.

All emotions have a positive intent. Emotional intelligence means understanding that emotions should *inform* your thoughts and actions in a helpful way, not make you feel bad for having them!

How to change your beliefs about emotions

Learning how to change the way you think about emotions is one of the most beneficial skills for becoming more emotionally intelligent. This does not mean changing the *emotion* – it's about changing the *way you think* about emotions.

Thinking in new ways is not as difficult as you might imagine provided the new ways are constantly repeated. How come? It's all down to your plastic brain!

Brain plasticity – or neuroplasticity, as it is also known – is the lifelong ability of the brain to change itself based on new experiences and new ways of thinking. The core components of the brain are neurons; cells in the nervous system that process and transmit information. The interconnections between neurons mean that, when you do something new, you create new connections, or pathways. It is like walking through a field of long grass, each step helping to create a new path.

If you change how you think or what you do, then new pathways are formed. When you continue using these new pathways, they become stronger and deeper. Eventually, they will replace the old ways of thinking and behaving; the old ways (or paths) will weaken and fade.

So just how can you practise thinking differently about emotions? Start by changing the way you think in other ways, unrelated to emotions.

Choosing to break a routine way of doing things on a regular basis can be a powerful way to help change your thinking.

brilliant tip

Move the kitchen bin to a different place in the kitchen. Or put the clock in a different place in the room. How long do you think it will take you to stop looking in the wrong place for the bin or the clock? Probably less than two weeks. Only two weeks to establish, with practice, a new way of thinking and behaving. Only two weeks to re-shape your brain!

Some people make a conscious effort to be flexible in their thinking about a range of issues and events, not just their emotions. They walk a different route round the supermarket or they walk a different route to work. They try out a new author or musician or a foreign language movie. One woman I know swapped her heels for trainers once a week – a real challenge to her comfort zone! By changing or breaking even small routines, your brain will be exposed to new stimuli and will create new neural pathways to accommodate changes.

You have to decide to do things differently to experience different results. What new things could you do? Start today: create new pathways in your brain. Get used to changing the way you think.

Sure, it's not easy to change the way you think, but it is not impossible. If you really are motivated to make a change, you will be more likely to focus on the *positive* aspects. And, if you focus on the positive aspects of change, you will be more inclined to make those changes. It's a win–win situation!

Positive thinkers recognise that all emotions have a positive intent. Thinking positively about emotions allows you to feel in control of your life and believe there is something you can do to manage your emotions, feelings and behaviour.

And, as a bonus you'll find that 'negative' emotions make fewer appearances to be reckoned with!

So, train your brain to think positive. Below are some of the most effective strategies.

Count your blessings – and be grateful

Positive thoughts are, of course, inherent in gratitude because when you think about the good, positive things that have happened, you are using the positive thinking pathways in your brain.

The smallest things can make the biggest difference. However seemingly insignificant, gratitude happens even when you notice the small pleasures around you. Even if you have a pretty rubbish day, instead of focusing on the negative, get in the habit of identifying and reflecting on the small pleasures instead. Maybe the sun was shining? You got an amusing text from a friend? You had something nice to eat? Just make an effort for a couple of weeks to identify the good things in your day. After a while, it will become second nature. Often, people who identify and appreciate positive events even sleep better; they think fewer negative thoughts, and more positive ones, just before going to sleep. No matter what happened that day, they go to bed happy.

> the smallest things can make the biggest difference

So, before you go to bed each night, identify three good things that have happened during the day. You may simply reflect on what those things are while you are getting ready for bed. You could even write them down in a notebook, or blog and keep an ongoing record of all the positive experiences in your life.

However you do it, it's a simple but powerful technique for increasing your gratitude and developing positive thoughts.

Identify and spend time with the positive people in your life

People are either drains or radiators. The drains suck the life out of you. The radiators emanate warmth and make you feel good. While it's not always possible to cut the negative people out of your life, you can identify and spend more time with the radiators; the positive people. These are people who make you laugh, people who have a positive outlook, people who encourage you. Say thank you; thank those in your life who make it better and happier.

Do kind acts for others

Helping other people and doing kind acts for other people gets you into a cycle of positive thinking and behaviour. Doing something to benefit someone else can make you and the other person feel good.

Identify your successes

Identify and write down situations where you have managed emotions (yours or someone else's) successfully in the past. Remind yourself of these times as a way of helping you to manage similar situations in the future.

Use words that evoke strength and success

Collect positive words. Make an effort to use words such as enjoy, pleased, good, glad, kind, happy, thrilled.

Enjoy yourself

Films, TV programmes, music, food, exercise, sport, sunshine, spending time in the country. Know what makes you feel positive and happy and do more of it!

Accept emotions

Another way to think differently about emotions is simply to *accept* emotions. This means that instead of trying to suppress an emotion or feed an emotion with stress inducing thoughts, you simply understand that you or someone else *does* feel this way; this emotion *has* surfaced.

No matter how hard you try, you cannot bury or rid yourself of emotions like fear, anger, sadness, happiness and joy; they are pretty much hard wired into you.

Once you are more able to *accept* emotions as they arise, you will have taken another step to developing your emotional intelligence.

↗ exercise 2 Accepting emotions

Take a step back and see emotion from a distance. Rather than judging your emotions as good or bad, simply feel and observe them. This is different from dissociating yourself from or denying the emotion, it's seeing your emotion from a little bit of a distance.

Mindfully observing an emotion can be done when you are experiencing an emotion that is strong enough that you recognise it, but not so strong that you are feeling overwhelmed by it.

The first step is to identify the emotion you are having. Stop for a moment and pay attention to your physical sensations and thoughts. See if you can give an emotion you are having a name; sadness? Jealousy? Shame? Instead of thinking, for example, 'it's not fair', an objective, mindful observation might take this form: 'Hmm, envy and resentment are present.'

See the emotion for what it is without judging it or attempting to get rid of it. Does it have a size and a shape? Does it have a colour?

Once you've done this, take a moment to reflect on what you noticed about your experience. What about changes in your reactions to the emotion? Did the emotion feel different in some way once you'd put some distance between you and the emotion?

Possibly not. So practise doing this every day for a couple of weeks. It won't take much time out of your day. After two weeks, see if you notice any changes in how you think about emotions. This exercise may seem a little strange at first, but people often notice that observing feelings and emotions in this way loosens their grip and allows them to see emotions as separate entities. It's also a helpful way to test out a belief that 'my emotions will get out of control if I don't try to push them out of my mind'.

brilliant recap

- Your ideas and beliefs about emotions are established quite early in life.

- If you've learnt to believe that a particular emotion is 'wrong' in some way and you try to ignore or deny an emotion, you cut off the message that the emotion is trying to convey.

- Denying, repressing and burying feelings does not get rid of them. Instead, when emotions are buried, they leak out in other ways.

- You *can* replace unhelpful beliefs about emotions with more helpful and empowering beliefs. Following the exercises, tips and techniques in this chapter can help you change your mindset.

- Thinking positively about emotions will help you to feel in control of your life and believe there is something you can do to manage emotions, feelings and behaviour.

CHAPTER 4

Identify and understand emotions

When you look at other people's faces it's possible to discover a range of information about them. Not just general information like their gender and age but also more specific information; their mood and what they're feeling.

It would appear that in widely disparate cultures, people express and interpret six basic emotions – fear, sadness, happiness, disgust, surprise and anger – in much the same way. All people in all parts of the world use these same expressions; they frown when they're angry for example, and smile when they're happy.

Remember, we have emotions for a good reason. Imagine, for example, if you were unable to recognise the emotion of fear; you'd be leaving yourself open to potentially harmful situations. On the other hand, when you respond appropriately; freeze, flee or confront the source of the fear, you are more likely to protect yourself.

So, while it's not a very pleasant emotion, fear *is* essential. Along with the other basic emotions of anger, happiness, sadness, disgust and surprise, fear is a clear emotion with clear signals.

Often though, we end up with a vague, confusing emotion. For example, you may have an experience which leaves you thinking 'I feel awful!' Awful is not an emotion, but it may be the closest you get to describing how you feel.

By not knowing what you are feeling, your emotions may feel very unpredictable and out-of-control. On the other hand, being able to identify emotions more clearly will help you to more easily understand, anticipate and manage feelings and behaviour. Although it takes practice, it is never too late to learn to identify and understand emotions.

Let's not forget that the little emotions are the great captains of our lives and we obey them without realizing it.

Vincent Van Gogh

Let's start quite simply – with a list of emotions. It's not an inclusive list, it's simply to help you be aware of the many emotions there are.

Affection	Euphoria	Misery
Anger	Excitement	Panic
Anguish	Fear	Passion
Annoyance	Frustration	Pleasure
Anxiety	Gratitude	Pride
Apathy	Grief	Rage
Awe	Guilt	Regret
Boredom	Happiness	Remorse
Contempt	Hate	Sadness
Curiosity	Hope	Satisfaction
Desire	Horror	Shame
Despair	Hostility	Shock
Disappointment	Hurt	Shyness
Disgust	Hysteria	Sorrow
Dread	Indifference	Suffering
Ecstasy	Joy	Surprise
Embarrassment	Loathing	Terror
Envy	Love	Wonder
		Worry

There are, of course, many emotions and many words to describe emotions. People who have a large vocabulary of names for feelings are often better able to express their emotions using language, rather than behaviour.

What, for example is the word for the feeling of unhappiness that happens after something you'd hoped for or expected, didn't in fact happen? It's disappointment. In what way does it differ from regret? Regret focuses on the choices a person made that contributed to a poor outcome, while disappointment focuses on the outcome itself.

Which words do you usually use to describe how you're feeling? Look up the definitions of those words in a dictionary or on a website such as www.dictionary.reference.com. Do you agree with the definitions? Do they accurately reflect how you feel when you use those words to describe how you're feeling?

Be aware that words describing emotions might not be the same for everyone. For example, happiness has a buoyant meaning for most people. However, for others, happiness relates to feeling unstressed and that nothing is bothering them. For these people, happiness has a quiet, calm meaning.

> words describing emotions might not be the same for everyone

brilliant tips

- If you have young children or work with children, give them words for their feelings and emotions. Start with simple terms such as angry, sad, happy or frightened, then move beyond these basic feeling words to less simple, more complex ones, such as lonely, excited, frustrated and grateful.

- For yourself, experiment with expressing emotions that you don't usually express. For example, if you never admit to feeling envious, when it's relevant in a conversation, describe an experience of envy you have had.

- Emotional Charades is a game that you can play with children to introduce the idea of a wide range of emotions. It's also a good party game for grown ups! Start by writing different emotions on pieces of paper and place them in a bowl. Have each person choose a piece of paper with an emotion, then, using facial expressions, gestures and body language the person has to convey that emotion while the other people try to guess correctly. This is a great game, because it helps everyone learn how to be more aware of feelings and how to better read people. If a child can look at someone's body and face and be aware of what they might be feeling, they'll have a skill for life!

Identify and own your feelings

Asking someone to do something for you, failing to get a particular job, seeing someone else achieve or acquire something that you wanted; these kinds of situations all have feelings attached to them.

Try noticing how you *feel* about the situation. Anxious? Dismayed? Hurt? Jealous?

Don't be afraid to identify and own your feelings and emotions. They do not define you; they are simply temporary internal messages to yourself that can help you understand your motivations and actions.

If how you feel is a response to someone else's actions or behaviour, start by saying '*I* feel' and not '*you* are making me feel'. For example, saying, '*You* are making me angry' blames the other person for how you feel. On the other hand, saying, '*I* am feeling angry' is taking responsibility for feeling that way.

Rephrasing your feelings and owning them is a powerful way of discovering that it's ok to feel the way you do.

How would you rephrase the last four sentences, below?

You've embarrassed me ... I feel embarrassed

You've been dishonest ... I feel deceived

You're driving like an idiot ... I feel ...

You've lied to me ... I feel ...

You've disappointed me ... I feel ...

You've made me feel really small ... I feel ...

Rather than blame someone else for your emotions, being aware of how you feel can help you take responsibility and manage your feelings.

Emotional needs

Just as you can identify and take responsibility for your emotions, so you can also identify and take responsibility for your emotional *needs*. We are all born with essential physical and emotional needs. Physical needs are essentials like food, water, sleep, warmth and shelter. Emotional needs include:

- Feeling safe and secure.
- Having a sense of autonomy and control; to be able to make and implement choices.
- Self-respect and good levels of self-esteem.
- Having a sense of meaning, purpose and achievement. To feel competent and capable. To feel challenged and creative.
- Feeling emotionally connected to others – to feel that you are acknowledged, accepted, included and that you belong. To feel that you are understood valued and respected. To feel liked, loved, admired, appreciated, approved of, cared for and needed. To feel trusted, supported and, when appropriate, forgiven.

- Having a spiritual connection – a connection to something bigger than ourselves.

While we all have emotional needs, each of us differs in the strength of the need, just as some of us need more water, more food or more sleep.

One person may need more of a sense of achievement; another may need more acceptance and admiration.

brilliant example

Identifying emotional needs

Rather than blame someone else for your unmet emotional needs, identifying your emotional needs can help you take responsibility for meeting those needs.

For example: *When I am feeling lonely, I have an emotional need for connection.*

Fill in the blanks to the sentences below.

When I am feeling bored I have an emotional need for ...

When I am feeling guilty, I have an emotional need for ...

When I am feeling unsure or uncertain, I have an emotional need for ...

Take your time

Once emotions have come to the surface identify them and be clear about how you feel. What if you're not sure about how you feel? Don't panic! There are a range of situations where you might not be clear about how you feel or your feelings are overwhelming you.

Take a minute to think about it. Take time to engage the thinking part of your brain and be aware that how you feel about a particular situation can help you respond in an emotionally intelligent way.

brilliant tip

To practice identifying emotions, read novels, biographies and autobiographies, watch dramas and soap operas. Compare the reactions and motivations of the characters with your own reactions and motivations. That's not to say that there's a right and wrong, this is just to raise your awareness at identifying emotions and tracing where they come from.

If a character is confused or sulking, for example, what emotions do you think are behind his or her thinking and actions?

To take it a step further, watch debate programmes, interviews on the news etc. and try to pinpoint the emotion underlying people's beliefs, expectations and opinions.

Be aware of the nonverbal communication; the gestures, facial expressions, tone of voice etc. that are associated with that emotion. (More on this in Chapter 5.)

Understanding emotions

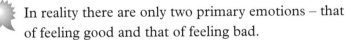

In reality there are only two primary emotions – that of feeling good and that of feeling bad.

Cecilia d'Felice

To help analyse and understand emotions more clearly, psychologists and researchers have attempted to categorise emotions. There is not, though, one specific way of categorising them; theorists disagree even on what the basic emotions are.

Some would say that there are just two basic emotions; happiness and fear – one is desirable and pleasant, the other is undesirable, unpleasant and gives pain - and that all other emotions are derived from these two emotions.

So, for example, anxiety, guilt, anger, sadness, shame are all fear-based emotions. Trust, compassion, truth, contentment and satisfaction are happiness-based emotions.

> emotions can also be seen in terms of wanting and not wanting

Emotions can also be seen in terms of wanting and not wanting. You have emotions about what you want and you have emotions when you don't get what you want. Then, when you have what you wanted, you have emotions about what you've got!

- Emotions of wanting: hope, anticipation, desire, envy, greed.
- Emotions of not wanting: fear, anxiety, shame, disgust.
- Emotions of having: happiness, pride, guilt, jealousy.
- Emotions of not having: sadness, distress, anger.

Another simple way of thinking about emotions is to see that emotions reflect the positive and negative assessments we make about the past, present and future.

	Past or present	Future
Positive	Happiness. Gratitude. Relief	Hope. Optimism. Excitement
Negative	Guilt. Regret. Embarrassment	Anxiety. Fear. Vengeance

So happiness is a fairly broad emotion that comes from the realisation that something pleasant and positive has happened or is happening. Gratitude is a more specifically focused emotion; it's a response to something good that has happened, for example, when someone else has done you a favour.

Hope concerns the future – it is the understanding that something good may happen. Excitement is an emotion that involves looking forward to something that is definitely going to happen.

Anxiety can be a broadly focused emotion that occurs when you expect something negative to come your way. Vengeance is a much more specifically focused emotion.

Guilt occurs as a result of realising you've done or are doing something wrong and has feelings of shame attached. Regret is also focused on the past but differs from guilt in that it doesn't come with value judgements.

These explanations help to show that emotions are linked in some way; that they are related and can be categorised.

One way of categorising emotions that clearly shows the relationships between them comes from psychology professor W. Gerrod Parrott in his book *Emotions in Social Psychology*.[1] Parrott's list of emotions and way of categorising them takes into account the relationships and interdependence of emotions, rather than seeing each emotion as separate. Parrott suggests that there are 6 basic emotions, 25 secondary emotions and 134 tertiary emotions; 165 emotions in all.

So, for example, for Parrott, both guilt and disappointment stem from the primary emotion of sadness. If we accept that *sadness* is characterised by feelings of loss and helplessness, Parrott suggests that guilt and disappointment are rooted in feelings of loss and helplessness.

Looking at emotions in this way helps us, first, to understand the deeper emotion that's behind or underpinning the secondary or tertiary emotion. It also allows us to understand which basic emotions may lead to experiencing a variety of secondary and tertiary emotions.

Primary emotion	Secondary emotion	Tertiary emotions
Love	Affection	Adoration, affection, love, fondness, liking, attraction, caring, tenderness, compassion, sentimentality
	Lust	Arousal, desire, lust, passion, infatuation
	Longing	Longing
Joy	Cheerfulness	Amusement, bliss, cheerfulness, gaiety, glee, jolliness, joviality, joy, delight, enjoyment, gladness, happiness, jubilation, elation, satisfaction, ecstasy, euphoria
	Zest	Enthusiasm, zeal, zest, excitement, thrill, exhilaration
	Contentment	Contentment, pleasure
	Pride	Pride, triumph
	Optimism	Eagerness, hope, optimism
	Enthralment	Enthralment, rapture
	Relief	Relief
Surprise	Surprise	Amazement, surprise, astonishment
Anger	Irritation	Aggravation, irritation, agitation, annoyance, grouchiness, grumpiness
	Exasperation	Exasperation, frustration
	Rage	Anger, rage, outrage, fury, wrath, hostility, ferocity, bitterness, hate, loathing, scorn, spite, vengefulness, dislike, resentment
	Disgust	Disgust, revulsion, contempt
	Envy	Envy, jealousy
	Torment	Torment
Sadness	Suffering	Agony, suffering, hurt, anguish
	Sadness	Depression, despair, hopelessness, gloom, glumness, sadness, unhappiness, grief, sorrow, woe, misery, melancholy
	Disappointment	Dismay, disappointment, displeasure
	Shame	Guilt, shame, regret, remorse
	Neglect	Alienation, isolation, neglect, loneliness, rejection, homesickness, defeat, dejection, insecurity, embarrassment, humiliation, insult
	Sympathy	Pity, sympathy

Primary emotion	Secondary emotion	Tertiary emotions
Fear	Horror	Alarm, shock, fear, fright, horror, terror, panic, hysteria, mortification
	Nervousness	Anxiety, nervousness, tenseness, uneasiness, apprehension, worry, distress, dread

What we usually notice first are the surface emotions – the tertiary emotions. The primary emotions are often more intense and buried deeper. For example, if you felt mortified about something you had done, it's unlikely that you'd also recognise that feeling as stemming from fear.

With Parrott's way of explaining how emotions are linked, the fear involved is maybe the fear of being ridiculed or ostracised that underlies feeling mortified.

Parrott also links the secondary emotion of envy to the primary emotion of anger, and the tertiary emotion of jealousy. Anger can be seen as the result of a perceived lack of control or power over something that's important to you. Jealousy is slightly different from envy as it involves a third party and is about loss. Envy is always about potential gain. If someone else has achieved or gained possession of something that you want or haven't got, this could result in a feeling of not having any control or power over that particular issue.

Of course, it's possible that any of these emotions can combine with any of the others to produce a completely unique feeling and response in you or anyone else!

Plutchik's wheel of emotions

Another way of categorising emotions and seeing how they are related is Robert Plutchik's wheel of emotions.[2] It consists of eight basic, primary emotions and eight advanced emotions. Each advanced emotion is composed of two basic ones.

Plutchik's idea is related to a colour wheel; in the same way that primary colours blend to create other colours, *primary emotions* combine to form a complete spectrum of human emotions. For example, anger and disgust could combine to create contempt. A blend of joy and anticipation could result in optimism.

Each emotion varies in its intensity, ranging from very mild to intense. For example:

- Joy can move to serenity and to ecstasy.
- Trust can move to acceptance and to admiration.
- Fear can move to apprehension and to terror.

Plutchik also suggested that primary emotions can be understood in terms of pairs of polar opposites:

- Surprise is the opposite of anticipation.
- Sadness is the opposite of joy.
- Trust is the opposite of disgust.
- Fear is the opposite of anger.

You can view the wheel of emotions at http://aarronwalter. com/2011/06/24/robert-plutchiks-matrix-of-emotions.

exercise 3 Understand emotions; make links

What emotions have you felt or seen in other people in the last week or two? Does Parrott's way of categorising emotions give you a clearer understanding of the intent, motivations and behaviour underlying those emotions? In what way and what context do secondary and tertiary emotions lead to the primary emotion?

Does the tracing back to the primary emotion explain anything about the person's behaviour, motivations or responses?

What about Plutchik's wheel of emotions? Does the combination of sadness and surprise suggest disapproval to you? Is love the combination of joy and trust? How about the other combinations?

So, although there is no one single, definitive way of categorising emotions, all of these categories help us to identify and understand about what emotions there are, how they're related and how they differ.

Understand cultural differences

People all over the world see emotions as pleasant or unpleasant. They also experience basic emotions in the same way. For example fear is as an unpleasant feeling and happiness is always a pleasant desirable feeling. But, for other emotions, the way they are experienced, the responses they provoke and the way they are received and interpreted by others is not the same in all cultures. It all depends if the emotion is perceived as either advantageous or detrimental to not just the individual person's aims and well-being, but also other people's.

How come? Well, in general, cultures can be seen as collectivist and individualist. Individualist cultures, such as those of Western Europe and the United States, encourage and value individual effort and achievement. Collectivist cultures, such as those of Japan and Korea, emphasise and value family, community and group work.

In individualistic cultures, people think of themselves as individuals with a separate identity from other people. In individualistic societies, emotions are seen as a unique personal experience. It is assumed that individual people have different individual emotional worlds, and react in different ways to the same experiences.

On the other hand, in collectivist cultures, emotions reflect the outer, rather than the inner world and are seen as objective: it is expected that all people experience the same emotion in a given social situation.

In individualistic cultures the focus is on the positive or negative effect that an emotion has on the individual's internal state. But in collectivistic cultures the focus is on the extent to which the emotion reflects external matters – adhering to social norms or fulfilling one's duties.

So, the same situation might lead to different responses in collectivistic and in individualistic cultures.

brilliant example

In 2003, a study on the emotion of shame – the awareness of having done something dishonourable or inappropriate – investigated how shame is experienced and responded to by salespeople in Holland – an individualistic culture – and the Philippines – an interdependent, collectivist culture.[3]

Researchers discovered that although shame is experienced by people in both cultures in the same way – as a painful, self-conscious emotion – there was a difference in how people *behaved* as a result of experiencing shame.

It was found that for Dutch sales employees, a shameful episode was followed by a decrease in sales, poor communication and interpersonal skills. It would appear that this was because the employees directed most of their rationalising and reasoning inwards in a defensive way.

Conversely, shame experienced by Filipino sales employees resulted in the opposite effect; better sales, communication and interpersonal skills. The Filipino sales employees focused on rebuilding relationships and increasing sales. In collectivistic cultures, shame is an indication that social harmony has been damaged and that it's the individual's responsibility to rebuild it.

Are your emotions influenced by how an event affects you or by how it affects your group – your family, friends or colleagues? For example, if at work your team achieves something together they might each feel pride as a result of the shared effort and success, while an individual who achieves something might feel smug!

brilliant recap

- Although it's not difficult to recognise basic emotions like fear, anger, sadness, disgust, surprise and joy – there are many other emotions that aren't so easy to recognise or understand.

- Look up the definitions of feelings in a dictionary. Do the definitions accurately reflect how you feel when you use those words to describe how you're feeling?

- Take a minute to engage the thinking part of your brain and be aware of how you feel about a particular situation. This can help you respond in an emotionally intelligent way.

- Owning and taking responsibility for your emotions and emotional needs is an effective way of accepting that it's ok to feel the way you do.

- Being aware of the links and relationships between emotions will help you to understand them more clearly.

- Apart from the six basic emotions, the way emotions are experienced, the behaviour they provoke and the way emotions are interpreted by others is not the same in all cultures.

CHAPTER 5

Nonverbal emotions

dentifying, using and managing nonverbal communication is an important aspect of emotional intelligence. Facial expressions, posture, touch etc. are all emotionally driven. Nonverbal messages can create, for example, a sense of interest, trust and empathy between people or they can generate fear, confusion, distrust and apathy.

> nonverbal communication is a natural language that conveys your true feelings and intentions

Nonverbal communication is a natural, mostly unconscious language that conveys your true feelings and intentions in any given moment, and clues you in to the feelings and behaviour of other people. So, if you want to develop your emotional intelligence, it makes sense to be more aware of nonverbal behaviour.

Nonverbal communication awareness strengthens emotional intelligence because it helps you to:

- Recognise a range of emotions, gauge moods and be more likely to know when others are feeling, for example, anxious, bored, embarrassed or pleased, more easily than if you just listen to what others say.

- Identify contradictions between what is being said and what that other person might really be thinking and feeling.

- Respond in ways that show others that you understand, notice and care.
- Know that what you say is consistent with how you feel.
- Manage difficult situations; you can use nonverbal communication to support or moderate a situation.

Where does nonverbal communication originate from?

Nonverbal communication originates in the most primitive part of your brain – your limbic brain. It's the area of your brain that reacts to other people, events and the world around you in a spontaneous and genuine way. It's also where your emotions spring from; emotions that occur automatically, without rational thought or reasoning.

Limbic (emotional) responses are hard wired into your system, which makes them difficult to control – like trying to suppress a smile when something amuses you.

Another part of your brain, the neo cortex – the new brain – is responsible for thinking, remembering and reasoning. It is this area that gives you the ability to think about and understand the emotions, intentions and behaviour of both yourself and others.

Because *verbal* communication is mostly conscious and intentional, you use the neo cortex part of your brain to formulate, control and express in words your thoughts, feelings, ideas and opinions.

In contrast, nonverbal communication is mostly unconscious and unintentional. So, just as the means of communication for the rational mind is words, the means of communication for the emotions is mostly nonverbal.

Because you are usually unaware how much you are conveying nonverbally, nonverbal messages often reveal your thoughts, feelings and emotions more genuinely than what you say. And when you are interacting with other people, you are reading or picking up on *their* nonverbal communication without being aware of it.

(Intuition is actually this unconscious process of tuning in to and responding to nonverbal information. See Chapter 1.)

All of our nonverbal behaviours are expressed in the way we listen, look, move and react. The gestures we make, the way we sit, how fast or how loud we talk, how close we stand, how much eye contact we make, all send strong messages about how we're feeling.

Any emotion, if it is sincere, is involuntary.

Mark Twain

The 7 per cent–38 per cent–55 per cent rule

How often have you been told that communication is 55 per cent body language, 38 per cent tone of voice, 7 per cent words? In fact, this isn't entirely accurate.

Professor Albert Mehrabian, whose work is the source of these statistics, certainly did not make such a sweeping claim. He has stated that: 'My percentage numbers apply only when a person is communicating about *emotions* and definitely do not apply to communication in general' (personal communication).

So, it's the communication of *emotions and feelings* that is made up of 7 per cent what is said, 38 per cent tone of voice, 55 per cent body language. That means that 93 per cent of yours and other people's *emotions and feelings* are communicated nonverbally.

Why nonverbal communication matters

When your nonverbal communication reflects the words you're saying, it can create trust, clarity and rapport. On the other hand, there are times when what you say in words and what your body language communicates appear to be two totally different things. When faced with mixed messages, other people either focus on your nonverbal messages (as Professor Mehrabian suggests) or the conflicting messages create confusion and distrust for the other person.

brilliant example

Sanjeev and Naomi are both articulate speakers but their nonverbal communication and ability to read other people's body language lets them down.

In meetings Sanjeev is keen and interested, he listens to other people's thoughts and opinions and often comes up with some great ideas. But, people tend to avoid talking on a one to one basis with him. If you were to ask why, Sanjeev's colleagues would say that he is 'too intense'. 'He stands too close and stares at you when you talk with him', says Abi, one of his colleagues. 'He touches your arm too often but when you back away to regain a more comfortable distance, he just steps nearer again.'

Naomi is well thought of at work; she is experienced, efficient and skilled at what she does. However, she radiates tension. Her shoulders and eyebrows are often noticeably raised, her body is tense and her voice is squeaky. People often feel uneasy and uncomfortable being around Naomi.

Although well intentioned, both Naomi and Sanjeev struggle to connect with others. Neither of them are aware of, first, the impact of the nonverbal messages they communicate and, second, of other people's nonverbal reactions.

To communicate effectively, avoid misunderstandings and enjoy positive relationships both socially and professionally, it's important they understand both how to use and interpret other people's nonverbal signals

Read the statements below. Which statements are true? Which ones are false?

1   An upward roll of the eyes signals frustration or exasperation.

2   If you see a person biting their lip, he or she is anxious or stressed.

3   A tight lipped smile suggests that the other person dislikes or distrusts you.

4   Chin up shows courage.

Answer: while these nonverbal behaviors *can* indicate specific feelings and emotions body language is more subtle than you might think. For example, someone biting their lips could be stressed or anxious. But it could just mean that they are concentrating on something. A person standing with their chin up could signal courage but in could also signal pride or defiance.

> body language is more subtle than you might think

Types of nonverbal communication and body language

Nonverbal communication usually supports, moderates or emphasises verbal communication (speech dependent) it can also be used on its own (speech independent) to communicate attitudes, emotions and feelings.

Nonverbal communication plays several roles:

● **Supporting**: nonverbal communication can add to or complement a verbal message. Briefly touching the arm of someone who is upset at the same time as expressing words of concern can increase the impact of the message.

● **Emphasising**: nonverbal communication can underline a verbal message. Pounding the table, for example, can emphasise an urgent point you're making.

moderating: nonverbal communication can reduce the impact or intensity of a verbal message. For example, smiling if you wanted to communicate that although you'd just expressed dislike about something, it was not the fault of the other person.

- **Contradiction**: nonverbal communication can contradict a message the individual is trying to convey – for example, when someone says something serious but winks to convey that they don't really mean it.

- **Substitution**: nonverbal communication can take the place of a verbal message. For example, pulling a face to show dislike or disgust.

Let's look at the many ways in which we all communicate nonverbally, so that you can use and understand these signs and signals to develop your emotional intelligence.

Facial expressions: eyes and mouth

The human face is able to express countless emotions without saying a word. Facial expressions for fear, anger, disgust, happiness, surprise and sadness are instantly recognisable. It's not too difficult either, for most of us to accurately determine the differences in facial expressions for, for example, irritation or worry, defiance or apology. To test yourself on this go to glennrowe.net/BaronCohen/Faces/EyesTest.aspx and see how well you manage to correctly identify a range of emotions.

Eye contact (or the lack of it) instantly sends a message. Whether it's a challenging, contemptuous stare, a look of fear, a loving gaze, a glazed over expression, before the first words are said you usually have a good idea what's coming next.

The mouth is a very flexible and expressive part of the face, performing a central role in many facial expressions. A mouth that is turned up or down can indicate a range of feelings.

Although a smile is one of the clearest nonverbal signals, smiles can be interpreted in many ways; it may be genuine, but a smile can also convey sarcasm, scepticism or cynicism.

↗ exercise 4 Reading facial expressions

Practise your ability to read and understand facial expressions; watch a drama, soap opera or film on a screen with the sound turned down. Because you're not distracted by the sound, this is a good way to read emotions, attitudes and feelings. What do the facial expressions of the people involved, tell you?

Doing this exercise is also a good way to develop your understanding, not just each individual person's attitudes and feelings, but also for increasing your understanding of the interactions between groups of people.

Head

A person's head has the ability to turn, jut forward, withdraw, tilt sideways, forwards, backwards. All of these movements have meanings which can convey, for example, like and dislike, acknowledgement, confidence, agreement and disagreement.

Gestures

Gestures can be some of the most direct and obvious nonverbal communication. Without thinking, we wave, point, beckon and use our hands to express ourselves. Gestures can be used in place of speech (speech independent) and have a direct verbal translation or gestures can be used together with spoken words (speech dependent).

Most speech *independent* gestures have specific meanings in particular cultures ranging from complimentary to highly offensive!

Giving a thumbs-up or a peace sign, for example, might have a completely different meaning in one culture to another. In another example, someone curling their index finger towards themselves in a summoning motion is a gesture used to beckon someone to follow them. However, in the Far East it's a method of communication considered worthy only to use with dogs!

Speech *dependent* gestures are used spontaneously when a person speaks and are used to support or emphasise what is being said. For example, when a person nods in the direction of something or someone they are talking about.

Posture

The way a person holds themselves, how they sit and stand and walk, their body orientation, direction of lean, position of their arms can convey a wealth of information about their emotions and how they're feeling about another person or situation.

With *open postures* the body is open and exposed. This type of posture generally indicates a person is feeling relaxed, calm, confident, engaged and is approachable.

Closed postures involve keeping the body obscured or hidden, often by hunching forward and keeping the arms and legs crossed. This type of posture may indicate more negative feelings of hostility, stress or pain.

Haptic communication

Haptics refers to touch as a form of nonverbal communication. We communicate a great deal through touch. This type of nonverbal communication can reveal intentions or feelings; for example, a limp handshake, a warm bear hug, a reassuring pat on the back, a patron-

we communicate a great deal through touch

ising pat on the head, or a controlling grip on your arm, can each signal a different attitude or emotion.

The meanings and intentions that are conveyed by touch are highly dependent upon the context of the situation, the relationship between people, and socially acceptable levels of touching.

Proxemics

The term proxemics refers to the distance between people as they interact. If you have ever felt uncomfortable during a conversation because the other person was standing too close and invading your space, then you'll know the impact that personal space can have between people.

Just as gestures, posture, touch etc. can communicate a great deal of nonverbal information, so can the physical space between people. Physical space can be used to communicate a variety of nonverbal messages, including aggression, dominance, or affection.

The amount of space and distance between us differs depending on the situation, personality characteristics, level of familiarity and what is culturally and socially acceptable.

Below are the four areas of personal space; public, social, personal and intimate, that, without thinking about, we typically respect and use in the UK.

- Intimate distance – 6 to 18 inches. Physical distance at this level between people usually indicates a close and comfortable relationship. It often occurs during intimate contact such as hugging, whispering or touching.
- Personal distance – 1.5 to 4 feet. This level of space usually occurs between people who are friends or family members and to separate people waiting in queues.

- Social distance – 4 to 12 feet. This level of distance is typically used between individuals who are acquaintances or strangers; in cases where you do not know the other person well or in public areas – shops and bus stops for example.
- Public distance – 12 to 25 feet. This is usually the distance maintained in a public speaking situation, between a speaker and the audience. For example, when teaching a class or giving a presentation at work.

Voice

It's not just what is said, it's *how* it's said that also matters. As well as listening to the words, people tune in/pick up on timing and pace, volume, tone and inflection, and sounds that convey understanding, such as 'uh-huh' or not understanding, 'er?'. Tone of voice, when saying 'Oh, that's great' for example, could indicate either sarcasm, enthusiasm, or confidence.

Making sense and meaning of nonverbal communication

The key to effective interpretation of nonverbal communication is to take into account *the context and the combination* of nonverbal signals.

First, taking context into account means taking into consideration all the seemingly unimportant circumstances that are, in fact, entirely relevant to what's happening. It is *these* supporting conditions that determine the meanings of the nonverbal messages we send and receive.

What is said in words, who else is there, current situation and circumstances, what's happened in the past are just some of the factors that contribute to context.

The second important thing to consider is that a *single verbal sign isn't as reliable as several signs*. Rather than interpret single gestures, facial expressions etc., the trick is to look for a *combination* of verbal and nonverbal communications and actions. Combinations of nonverbal communications provide a much more reliable indication of meaning than one or two gestures or expressions in isolation. So look out for several signs that all seem to be implying the same thing.

Children are a great example of this. Try insisting to a small child that he does something he doesn't want to do. The combination of saying 'no', scowling, stamping his foot, turning his back and hunching his shoulders will leave you in no doubt about how he feels!

brilliant tip

- Don't read too much into a single gesture or nonverbal cue. Take into account several verbal and nonverbal signs; facial expression, tone of voice and gestures.

- Know that each person has their own individual baseline behaviours; their usual way of acting and behaving. The key to using these nonverbal cues is to compare them with the person's normal behaviour - their baseline. If you are aware of what is natural and typical for someone you have something to compare it against and you will be more aware when something doesn't quite fit.

- Be aware of inconsistencies. Nonverbal communication should reflect or reinforce what is being said. Is the person saying one thing and their body language something else? For example, are they insisting they feel fine but they are avoiding eye contact and - unusually for them - biting their nails?

- Trust your instincts. If you get the sense that someone isn't being honest about how they feel or that something isn't adding

▶

up, you may be picking up on a mismatch between verbal and nonverbal communication.

- Look out for changes; a change in a person's emotions will be evident in their nonverbal behaviour.

- Be aware that behavioural, mental and physical difficulties can affect a person's nonverbal communication.

- Also remember that cultural differences influence body language signals and their interpretation. For example, you might be familiar with the gesture where a person touches their temple – the side of their head – with their index finger in order to indicate someone (or an action) is clever or intelligent. Touching the *forehead – the front of their head* – with the index finger means someone (or an action) is stupid or crazy. In Russia these meanings are reversed.

- Pay attention! If you are distracted in any way or thinking about something else, you are almost certain to miss nonverbal cues and other subtle cues that the other person may be conveying. Stay focused and mindful in order to fully understand what's going on.

- Don't get too caught up analysing the other person's body language and don't always assume that you have correctly identified the meaning of another person's body language. Do remember to listen and ask questions.

brilliant example

During a meeting at work, Arlene had suggested that, for a couple of reasons, the sales team feed back sales figures more regularly to the marketing team. Arlene's manager thought this would be a good move and asked Sid, the manager of sales, if he was ok with this. 'Yeah, sure', replied Sid. 'Great', said Arlene's manager, looking up from some papers on his desk. 'Not so great', thought Arlene. Sid's nonverbal communication contradicted his words. Apart from speaking through pursed lips, his facial expression was blank and as he spoke he turned his head away from Arlene and her manager. Arlene took this as a cue to suggest that before they move on, they discuss any difficulties her idea might pose. Sid sat forward and said 'Yes, actually. I can see a couple of problems.' 'Ok, let's discuss them now', said Arlene. Sid visibly relaxed and the meeting proceeded.

Setting the stage for effective nonverbal communication

Becoming more aware of and interpreting other people's body language also helps you to become more aware of your *own* nonverbal communication. Other people draw conclusions from your body language about your attitude and emotions; even if you are silent you are still communicating through your posture and facial expressions.

> even if you are silent you are still communicating through your posture and facial expressions

In certain situations, for example, a combination of minimal eye contact, pursing your lips and fidgeting might lead the other person to conclude that you are feeling irritated. In other situations a combination of actions – leaning slightly forward, head tilted to one side and briefly touching the other person's arm – can convey sympathy without you having to say a single word.

Here are some nonverbal signs and signals to be aware of.

Posture

Not only can your posture be influenced by how you feel, it also works the other way round; your posture can actually influence how you feel.

It will probably come as no surprise that if, for example, you are feeling intimidated or anxious, hunching and drooping gives away that you are ill at ease and chances are that others may feel just as uncomfortable around you!

But what message is your body language sending to other people? More importantly, what message is it *sending to your own brain*?

Psychologists have known for some time that your body language tells people a lot about you. But recent research confirms that the way you sit or stand actually affects the way your brain functions.[1,2] Carry yourself with confidence and in a matter of minutes your body will start to feel it and your brain will start to believe it.

In one study, psychologists asked participants to spend two minutes in one of two types of poses; either an open pose (leaning back in a chair, feet up on the desk, fingers laced behind the head, elbows out) or in a tight, closed pose (sitting with shoulders hunched, legs together, hands clasped in lap).[2] Remarkably, not only did the people who held expansive poses report feeling more confident than the others did but they also experienced a measurable physiological shift: their testosterone increased by 19 per cent, while their levels of the stress hormone cortisol fell by 25 per cent.

In contrast, those people who adopted the submissive poses showed a *decrease* in testosterone and an *increase* in cortisol.

Even when you are feeling intimidated or self-conscious you can convey feelings that you're not actually experiencing; you can positively influence how you feel by simply changing your posture. You don't have to learn a whole new repertoire of poses, gestures and expressions that feel unnatural or uncomfortable. If you can alter just one or two things consistently, the rest of your body and mind will catch up and you will feel more confident and come across as more confident and capable.

So, take a moment to think about what you are typically doing with your body when you are at work, socialising or with family members. If you sit all hunched up or stand with your arms tightly crossed you are going to end up feeling less confident and less in control because that's the message your brain will receive.

It's up to you to make sure your brain is getting the right message. If you want to feel more in control and confident, not just *appear* confident but genuinely feel confident, simply choose to do just two or three of these actions:

- stand or sit straight;
- keep your head level;
- relax your shoulders;
- spread your weight evenly on both legs;
- if sitting, keep your elbows on the arms of your chair (rather than tightly against your sides);
- make appropriate eye contact;
- lower the pitch of your voice;
- speak more slowly.

You can't control all your nonverbal communication; in fact the harder you try, the more unnatural your signals are likely to come across. So just use one or two.

If you can do one or two of those things consistently, your thoughts, feelings and the rest of your nonverbal signals will catch up. It's a dynamic process where small changes in how you use your body can add up to a big change in how you feel, how you behave and the impact you have on other people.

Try out your confident posture in front of the mirror and make yourself aware of what your 'confident me' looks and feels like.

Experiment with a range of behavioural styles, from the most dominant to the most deferential.

Leon needs to tell his manager Heidi that, for personal reasons, unless he can reduce his work time to three days a week, he will have to hand in his notice. He's feeling anxious.

Leon decides to focus on two things: maintaining eye contact and loosely clasping his hands with his elbows out slightly. 'Although I felt apprehensive, I kept eye contact, maintained the position of my hands and the rest of my mind and body started to follow. Unusually for me, I didn't gabble and trip over my words. It really helped me feel self-assured! I explained my situation and what I wanted calmly and clearly. Heidi listened to my concerns and said she'd talk to her manager and see what they could do.'

Although it's advisable to maintain a balanced posture, calm voice and gestures to help you look and feel confident, be aware that in other situations, faking a gesture or facial expression can come across as phony and insincere. When people say that someone seems false, they're usually referring to mannerisms that seem faked; they don't truly match what the speaker is saying.

This is because even when you deliberately try to control your body language, there is still what is known as 'leakage' that others can pick up. For example, your voice may 'leak' information about how you feel; although you are all smiles and try to appear pleased that someone else received the internal promotion you wanted, the disappointment in your voice leaks out when you offer your congratulations.

Distance and touch

Learn what is personally, socially and culturally acceptable in respect to touching other people. Make yourself aware of what the most comfortable distance between you and another person is in different situations.

In her living room, one of my family has the furniture arranged in such a way that there's a distance of about 15 feet between where she sits and the sofa where guests sit when they come to visit. This, for me at least, makes conversation feel awkward. So that we can sit at a more informal and relaxed distance, I usually ask to bring a chair in from the dining room and sit closer to her. It really does make all the difference.

Gestures

Are you aware of the gestures you normally use? Do you, for example, use your hands to provide a continuous physical interpretation of everything you say – like some news reporters and politicians – and detract from what you are saying?

Try to use calm, flowing hand movements rather than short sharp movements which can distract or intimidate the other person. On the one hand, try and avoid adopting new gestures that are not really you, but on the other hand, do use gestures selectively where they add the most impact.

Eyes

When somebody is speaking to you, even if you *are* following every word, are you *showing* that you're interested by making appropriate eye contact?

If you fail to make eye contact with the person who is speaking you may come across as being one of three things: bored, distracted or rude. And, if you're the one doing the speaking and are not making eye contact it could feel to the listener that they're not worth talking to or that you are not being honest and sincere in what you are saying.

There are times though, when face-to-face conversations with a high level of eye contact can inhibit communication. Sometimes a more relaxed approach is more effective. For example, if a conversation takes place when you are involved in an activity together.

brilliant example

Julie's father Stan is 65 and has lived on his own since his wife died 5 years ago. Stan is a quiet, reserved man and not very talkative. Whenever Julie pops in to visit Stan they sit opposite each other at the kitchen table and they soon run out of things to talk about. Julie didn't look forward to her visits.

Things changed though when Stan asked Julie to help him with the family tree. Julie discovered that in fact, they had lots to talk about when they were actually doing something together. The informality seemed to strike just the right note; natural and relaxed.

Paraverbal

Be aware that the tone, pitch, volume, inflection, rhythm and the speed that you speak all have an impact on what you say. These nonverbal speech sounds provide subtle but powerful clues to your true feelings, and intentions.

Keep things in perspective. Don't obsess about getting every aspect of your nonverbal behaviour 'right'. Other people will be picking up on a *combination* of your nonverbal behaviours. If you are being honest and sincere about what you're saying, the more likely it is that your nonverbal communication will reflect how you feel.

don't obsess about getting every aspect of your nonverbal behaviour 'right'

brilliant tip

Your body speaks your mind

Do you know when your body is telling you to take a break? Do you *listen* to your body? Or do you ignore it? When your body gives you information that you ignore, you lose out on valuable information that can let you know what is good for you and what isn't. That's not emotionally intelligent! So, tune into and act on the intuitive messages and insights that your body communicates to you.

brilliant recap

- Nonverbal communication conveys our true feelings and intentions.

- Up to 93 per cent of emotions and feelings are communicated nonverbally.

- Nonverbal communication originates in the your limbic brain. It's also where your emotions spring from; emotions that occur automatically, without thinking.

- The gestures you make, the way you sit, how fast or how loud you talk, how close you stand, how much eye contact you make, all send strong messages about how you're feeling.

- The key to effective interpretation of nonverbal communication is to be aware of the *context* and the *combination* of these nonverbal messages.

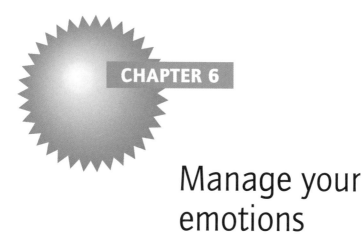

CHAPTER 6

Manage your emotions

So far in this book, you will have learnt that emotional intelligence means recognising, understanding and accepting emotions. The next step is to use your emotions to inform your responses, actions and behaviour. This does not mean *controlling* your emotions. It means being able to *manage* your emotions.

Controlling your emotions involves dominating, mastering, or suppressing your emotions. When you try to control your emotions then you are fighting against yourself. On the other hand, *managing* your emotions involves handling your emotions with a degree of skill and flexibility. You are working *with* yourself.

Remember, all emotions have a positive intent; *all* emotions are helpful in some way. Take sadness as an example. Sadness is characterised by feelings of loss and helplessness and looking inward. The positive intent of sadness is to help the person stay close to and adjust to what they have lost.

> *all* emotions are helpful in some way

So, start by asking yourself 'How are my emotions trying to help me?', instead of feeling like your emotions are controlling you or that you need to control them.

Manage your emotions using a variety of strategies

Managing your emotions involves developing a range of strategies with which to manage your response, behaviour and actions. Not every strategy works the same for every emotional experience. Research at Stanford University has shown that a flexible approach to managing emotions may be one key to emotional well-being and emotional intelligence.[1]

As you know, emotions vary in their intensity; some emotions have less strength and force and some are more powerful. The research has found that fitting the appropriate strategy with the intensity of the emotion will makes a difference to a person's ability to manage emotions and emotional situations.

For example, a reminder from a colleague about a mistake you recently made might leave you feeling irritated. On the other hand, your colleague questioning your ability to actually do your job would likely provoke a stronger emotional response!

Appraisal – which allows for emotional processing – is the most appropriate strategy when the emotional intensity is weak and you can easily rethink the situation.

On the other hand, when emotions are stronger they are not as easy to manage. This is because the part of your brain that springs into action when strong emotions occur is different from the area of your brain that operates when you are rationalising and reasoning. As a result, when you are very angry, disappointed or excited, for example, you cannot think or problem-solve.

Although strong emotions such as fear and surprise are usually temporary and last a relatively short time, strong emotions make thinking, rationalising and reasoning a real struggle. Instead, distraction, which tends to block and delay emotional processing is a more effective strategy. This doesn't mean permanently avoiding how you feel, it simply means turning your attention away and delaying your response.

So, if your colleague had questioned your ability to do your job and you had an important presentation to give in the afternoon, instead of allowing your anger to overwhelm you and undermine your ability to make the presentation, you distract yourself by focusing your attention on preparing for the presentation and maybe arrange something nice like meeting a friend for lunch.

In contrast, because irritation is a less overwhelming emotion, instead of being upset that your colleague has brought up your mistake, you can think through whether or not her remarks are fair and what you will or won't say or do about it.

In other words, you don't use a sledgehammer to crack a nut! Successful management of our emotions is all about picking the right strategy for the right situation. As Aristotle observed, what is wanted is appropriate emotion, feeling proportionate to circumstance.

 Feelings are much like waves, we can't stop them from coming but we can choose which one to surf.

Jonatan Mårtensson

Choose the right approach

Your emotions control you when you assume there's only *one* way to respond. But, you *always* have a choice.

For example, imagine you were driving in your car and someone pulled out in front of you on their bike. You hit the brakes and narrowly avoided hitting the cyclist. You might feel angry and your immediate response might be to get out of your car and start haranguing him or her. But no matter what the emotion, there are always alternative ways to behave. Rather than confront the other person, you *could* choose to let out your anger by swearing loudly once you had some distance between yourself and the cyclist.

In Chapter 3 you will have read that how you think *about* emotions can affect your emotional intelligence.

Remember also, that emotions are made up of physical feelings, thoughts and behaviour. Each of these aspects of an emotion can influence the other aspects. So, your thoughts about a *situation* can influence your feelings and your behaviour. There are helpful and unhelpful ways of reacting to most situations, depending on how you think about them. You *do* have a choice!

For example, imagine that you are walking down the road and someone you know walks by and appears to ignore you.

Aspects of an emotion	Unhelpful	Helpful
Thoughts	He deliberately ignored me. He doesn't like me.	I'm not sure that he saw me. I wonder if he was ok?
Physical feelings	Tense	Neutral
Behaviour	Do nothing, or go after him and confront him.	Catch up with him or phone/text later and enquire if he's ok.

The same situation has led to two very different responses, depending on how you thought about the situation. How you think has affected how you felt and what you did. In the example in the left hand column, you've jumped to a conclusion without very much evidence for it – and this has probably not led to a very positive result.

The more aware you are and the more you understand your emotional chain reactions, the easier it is to manage the situation. Seeing emotions in terms of thoughts, physical feelings and actions makes it easier to see how they are connected and how they affect you.

Take your time

Taking time to engage the thinking part of your brain and understand how you feel about a particular situation can help you see what choices you have in your response to a particular emotion and situation.

Imagine that your friend asked you to accompany her to see a singer whose music you can't stand. Your feelings of dread are telling you that you want to say no. But instead of taking a few seconds to notice how you feel (the fact that you started to feel tense should've been a clue!) and let your feelings inform your reply, you ignore your feelings and agree to go with her. Hardly an emotionally intelligent response, is it?

Or, you let your feelings take over and respond by exclaiming; 'You must be joking! No way am I going to sit through that crap. I can't think of anything worse than listening to that singer for two hours. I'd rather watch paint dry!'

Is there another, emotionally intelligent way to respond? Yes. *Think* before you speak; pause and give yourself a moment to think about what choice of responses you have.

brilliant tip

Change your physiology: breathe

Remember, emotions have physical aspects. So, part of managing your emotional state involves managing the physical aspects of your emotions.

Physical aspects can be influenced by the way you breathe. So if you are experiencing an emotion that includes increased heart rate and

▶

muscle tension, you might want to try a coping strategy that will bring those feelings down, such as slowing down your breathing. It might be advice you've heard before but it really can help.

- Stop breathing for five seconds (to 'reset' your breath).
- Now breathe in slowly for three seconds, then breathe out *even more slowly* (and whilst doing this, imagine that you are breathing pure calm into your hands).
- Keep doing this and remember it's the *out-breath* that will slow everything down.

Slowing breathing has an effect on the physical aspect of an emotion – it helps slow your heart rate.

Write the word 'pause' or 'breathe' on a sticky note. Place the note on your computer, near the phone or on the fridge to remind you to slow down, breathe and consider the alternative ways you have to respond.

Unless it's an emergency or an urgent situation that requires you to respond immediately and intuitively, make a choice. When deciding how to respond and what to do, pause and make a choice.

brilliant tip

Even when emotions are running high you *can* still engage the thinking part of your brain. You can do this by simply forcing yourself to recite the alphabet in your head, counting backwards from 20 or even remembering everything you had to eat and drink yesterday. Try it; it really will work.

Change your posture

As well as managing your breathing, you can also influence how you feel by simply changing your posture. If you can alter just one or two things consistently, the rest of your body and mind will catch up and you will feel more confident about managing your feelings and the situation. It's up to you to make sure your brain is getting the right message. Simply choose to do just two or three of these actions:

- stand or sit straight;
- keep your head level;
- relax your shoulders;
- spread your weight evenly on both legs;
- if sitting, keep your elbows on the arms of your chair (rather than tightly against your sides);
- make appropriate eye contact;
- lower the pitch of your voice;
- speak more slowly.

You can't control all your nonverbal communication but if you can do one or two of those things consistently, your thoughts, feelings and the rest of your nonverbal signals will catch up. It's a dynamic process where small changes in how you use your body can add up to a big change in how you feel and how you behave.

Move yourself

Physical exercise directly changes neurotransmitter activity in the brain. You don't have to go to the gym to influence how you feel – going for a walk, cleaning the house or your car and walking up a few flights of stairs will all help change your physiology and give you time to think, rationalise and reason.

Ask questions

Assuming you've managed your physical feelings, the next step is to manage your response. Try asking yourself a few questions first, to decide what response would be best.

- Shall I deal with the situation right now?
- What do I want – what do I want the outcome of this situation to be?
- What could happen if I respond by ...?
- What might happen if I don't respond in that way?
- What would help me feel better?
- Should I discuss this with someone before I do anything?
- What is the decision I'd feel proud of?

Asking these questions will help you to decide if you are ready to manage a situation right now, what your options might be and which approach is best.

brilliant example

Supposing, for example, you were extremely disappointed that you didn't get the internal promotion at work. You're also jealous of the person who did get the promotion.

- *Should I respond straight away?* Probably not. Probably not the best move to immediately hand in my notice.
- *What could happen if I do hand in my notice?* I'll feel pretty good. But then I'll regret it the next day.
- *What might happen if I don't?* Frustrated right now, but tomorrow, I'll be glad I didn't hand in my notice.
- *Should I discuss it with someone else?* Definitely. I'll talk it over with my partner this evening.

- *What do I want to accomplish?* I want to know why I didn't get the promotion.

- *What is the decision I'd feel proud of?* To hold fire and discuss it with my partner. Tomorrow, to ask for feedback, see what future opportunities there are and start looking for a new job before I hand in my notice.

Pausing to think means that you are the one in control because you have thought through your options.

Find something positive about the situation

Trying to find a positive aspect of your situation often makes you look at things in a different way and improve your ability to manage. For example, you might not have got the promotion and although the person who did get promoted is someone you don't like, at least it means they'll be leaving your department and you won't be working with them anymore. And, you're going to be looking for a new job. So focus on that.

Learn from past experience

Think about another time when you felt like this – disappointed, jealous, embarrassed etc. and it turned out ok in the end. What helped?

Write about it. Talk about it

If you like to write, write about how you feel. Write about your disappointment, your jealousy, your feelings of resentment; write about what happened and how you feel. You can write about the situation, how it affected you, how it made you feel. Write about how you reacted to this situation, what you said and what *you* did and what part you take responsibility for.

write emotions down and then plan a time to deal with them

If emotions are churning around inside your mind, write them down and then plan a time to deal with them. This externalises your thoughts – it empties your head and you can stop thinking, knowing that you'll deal with them later.

Talk or write to someone else

Another way to manage and release emotions is to tell someone else – a friend, colleague, family member, doctor, therapist. Choose wisely; talk to someone who's not directly involved and who *will* listen about what happened and how you feel.

Explain in detail what happened and your feelings around this experience. This will help you to release your feelings and gain a perspective on the situation. Be aware though, that if you keep repeating the story to different people, reliving all the anger, disappointment, hurt, or whatever the emotion might be over and over again, you are at risk of being defined by the emotion – resentful and bitter. The resentment then becomes another problem!

brilliant tip

Learn from other people. Who do you know that appears to successfully manage their emotions well? How do they deal with their frustrations and difficulties? You could even ask them: 'How do you keep calm when you're presenting to all these people? Or ' Why, when you're driving, don't you get angry when someone else pulls out in front of you?' Their answers could make a big difference to your life if you follow their strategies.

brilliant example

Nicola was feeling frustrated; once again, her colleague, Josh, was late for a meeting and this delayed the start of an important discussion. Nicola was aware that she was feeling frustrated. She was worried that a delayed start would cut down the time she had to deliver her sales pitch and that as a result, it would be less effective.

Nicola knew that it was important to deal with her feelings of frustration, otherwise she was at risk of making sarcastic remarks to Josh when he finally arrived which would make her look petty and unprofessional. She knew that the best thing she could do was to stop, take a few seconds and think what her options were. In other words, Nicola recognised that she had a choice.

First, Nicola changed how she felt. She concentrated on her breathing for one minute, to calm her heart rate and stop her feeling so tense.

Second, she changed her thinking. Nicola reframed the situation and tried to think of one positive thing about the situation. She figured that the delay at least gave her time to chat with others, which also distracted her from negative thoughts.

This small change in her thinking improved how she felt and helped her feel more in control.

Then, she reduced her frustration further by taking control. Nicola simply asked the chairperson if they could get started.

Finally, later that day, she spoke to Josh –'I felt really annoyed that you were late for the meeting. It cut the amount of time we had for our presentation; we had to rush it and it wasn't as good as it could've been.'

Managing your emotions involves handling your emotions with a degree of skill and flexibility. You need to manage each aspect of an emotion. Manage how you think, for example, and you

each aspect of an emotion can be influenced by another

will be more able to manage how you physically feel. You will then be more able to manage your response, actions and behaviour. Or, if you can manage how you physically feel, you'll be more able to manage your thoughts and behaviour. Each aspect of an emotion can be influenced by another.

Not every strategy works the same for every emotional experience, so develop a range of strategies; that's emotionally intelligent!

brilliant recap

- Emotional intelligence does not mean *controlling* your emotions. It means *managing* your emotions; handling your emotions with skill and a flexible approach.

- Your emotions control you when you assume there's only one way to respond. But you always have a choice.

- Managing your emotions involves developing a range of strategies with which to manage your response, behaviour and actions. Not every strategy works the same for every emotional experience.

- Remember that emotions are made up of physical feelings, thoughts and behaviour. Each of these aspects of an emotion can influence the other aspects.

- Manage how you think, and you will influence your physical feelings and your behaviour. Manage your physical feelings and you will be more able to manage your thoughts and behaviour. Manage your behaviour and you are more likely to manage your thoughts and physical feelings

CHAPTER 7

Manage other people's emotions

Strike the right emotional chord: develop empathy

Not only are people with high levels of emotional intelligence good at understanding and managing their own emotions they're good at understanding and managing other people. People with emotional intelligence are good communicators; they listen, know what to say and what not to say, when to say it and how. Typically, emotionally intelligent people are considerate and positive people, and this helps them to sense the emotional needs of others.

The key skill that you need to be one of these emotionally intelligent people is empathy.

Having empathy simply means that you are willing to try and understand someone else's situation, their point of view, their thoughts and feelings. You show interest in another person's situation and readiness to respond to their needs and feelings without dismissing or judging them.

You do not have to make the other person's situation your own or allow his or her feelings to dominate yours. Whether that person is feeling something that is about you or someone else, your aim is to *understand* his or her emotions, not be overwhelmed or undermined by them.

brilliant tip

Remember, the part of the brain that springs into action when strong emotions arise is different from the area of the brain that operates when a person is rationalising and reasoning. This means that when someone is angry, jealous, excited etc. they cannot think clearly. It's as if a wall has come down and they are behind it. This means that you are interacting with the emotion rather than the person. This is when you need to use emotional intelligence!

Having empathy means that you draw on your own understanding and experience of emotions and feelings to help relate to what others are saying and feeling, but keep in mind that the other person might feel or think differently than you do in any given situation.

brilliant example

Ruth is feeling increasingly irritated with her brother Simon. For the umpteenth time since he lost his job, Simon calls and complains endlessly in a 'poor me, life is so unfair' way.

Things change when Ruth changes her approach. Next time he phones she tries to imagine what Simon might be feeling – unhappy, anxious, resentful, fearful, overwhelmed? She's not clear so she asks 'Do you know what you want to do next or are you feeling overwhelmed? Simon confirms that he *is* feeling overwhelmed and doesn't know what to do; whether to rent out his house and take up a job abroad or wait it out for a job in the UK but risk being unable to pay his mortgage.

Ruth might not have been made redundant before, but she has experienced the same emotions Simon is feeling – being overwhelmed and uncertain. This puts Ruth in an empathic position; she can understand how Simon is feeling.

How empathy works

What gives us the ability to be empathic? Well, imagine that you see someone stub their toe on a chair. Immediately, in response, you also cringe. Or, you watch a horror film where a character in the film is terrified and *your* heart starts pounding and you hold *your* breath in dread.

This ability to quickly and easily understand what other people are experiencing has long puzzled neuroscientists and psychologists. But recent research has uncovered a fascinating explanation: brain cells called mirror neurons.

Mirror neurons are distinctive brain cells that fire, not just when *you* perform an action, but also when you see or hear *others* carry out an action, too.

Before the discovery of mirror neurons, in a series of studies by Rizzolatti, Di Pellegrino, Fadiga, Fogassi and Gallese at the University of Parma, Italy, in the early 1990s, it was thought that our brains used reason and rationalisation thought processes to make sense of other people's behaviour. Now, however, many researchers and scientists believe that we understand others not just by thinking, but by feeling.

It would appear that mirror neurons also allow you to interpret facial expressions; so when, for example, you see someone screw up their face in disgust at something that tastes awful, instinctively, you start screwing up your face in disgust, too. This is because the same regions of your brain become activated whether you are witnessing a specific expression from someone else, or making that expression yourself.

In fact, one study found that subjects who received Botox treatments that blocked their ability to mimic emotional expressions were subsequently less able to recognise others' emotions![1]

Not being able to see the other person's facial expressions might also account for the misunderstandings that can occur in written communication – letters, emails, texts etc. – where the element of immediate verbal feedback and facial expression is missing.

When you're smilin', when you're smilin', the whole world smiles with you.

Goodwin, Fisher and Shay

brilliant tip

Research into mirror neurons is providing new insights into the ways by which we communicate our feelings and intentions to each other.

The concept of mirror neurons has implications for 'catching' emotions. That's good when, for example, you see someone smile. Your mirror neurons for smiling are activated, too, creating a sensation in your own mind associated with smiling. You don't have to think about what the other person intends by smiling. You understand the meaning and smile back. The smile is infectious.

But, this also means that you can also 'catch' emotions such as anger, contempt and apathy from other people. When you are around others who are feeling like this, you can soon start to feel the same; tense, negative and miserable. (See the study below.)

Remember, you do not have to make their emotions your own or allow the other person's feelings to dominate yours. Using empathy, your aim is to *understand* the other person's emotions, not to get caught up in them.

The influence of other people's emotions

A study carried out in the 1960s showed that other people's behaviour can influence what emotion you think you are experiencing.[2]

Participants in the study were injected with adrenaline (supposedly to see how it would affect their vision) and were told the effect this would have on them. Some of them were told they would feel euphoric while others were told it would make them feel angry.

In fact all subjects experienced the same physical reactions to the drug, including increased heart rate, trembling and rapid breathing.

After the injection, each participant was then shown to a room (supposedly to wait for the adrenaline to kick in) where he or she encountered a person posing as another participant who had also been injected with the drug. If the first person had been told he or she would experience euphoria, then the second person – the stooge – would behave in a happy way and amuse himself with some of the items in the room – hoola hoops, pen, paper and rubber bands.

In the rooms where individual participants were told the adrenaline would make them feel angry, the stooge displayed angry behaviour by complaining about the 'tests' or storming out of the room.

Since the physical responses of both anger and euphoria are the same (increased heart rate, fidgety behaviour and rapid breathing), the injection worked in conjunction with the preconditioned mindset (anger or euphoria) to create a complete emotional experience.

Those who encountered the 'happy' stooge generally recorded their feelings as happy, while the participants who came in contact with the 'angry' stooge recorded negative feelings. The study shows how other people's emotions influence our own.

Develop empathy: listen

How can you increase your ability to be empathic and manage other people's emotions? The same way that you manage your own emotions – you start by *accepting* emotions. Accepting other people's emotions is a *passive* act; it means you do nothing but simply listen and observe. You don't judge, block, dismiss, take over, or allow the other person's feelings to dominate yours.

brilliant tip

Watch what happens when someone expresses emotion (guilt, shame or anger, for example) that is not directly about the person or people they are expressing it to. How do other people respond? Do they try to invalidate, ignore or block how the person is feeling and expressing their emotion? Do they 'catch' the emotion?

What are the most helpful and validating responses that you notice?

Next time you are with someone who expresses a strong emotion (whether it's about you or not – they might, for example, be furious that they've just received a parking ticket or they might be upset with you because you advised them that it was ok to park there) be attentive, without trying to reduce or stop their experience or expression of what they are feeling. Don't interrupt or ask questions, don't try to fix it, soothe them, offer solutions or, if it's about you, defend yourself. Instead, stop what you are doing and thinking and give them your full attention.

You might not agree with how they're feeling, but accepting how the other person feels goes a long way to validating the other person's emotions.

Nonverbal responses

Acceptance is mostly conveyed through your nonverbal responses. When someone is talking to you, they will be aware, albeit unconsciously, whether or not they are being listened to by your nonverbal responses.

Nonverbal acceptance and acknowledgement can be something as simple as a facial expression that reflects how the other person is feeling (those mirror neurons kicking in!), making eye contact, a nod of the head or a smile. Nonverbal acceptance can also be profound: a gentle touch, a sympathetic look or a thumbs up can convey empathy in ways that words cannot.

Be an active listener: acknowledge and show understanding

Having shown that you *accept* what the other person feels, the next step is to show that you are trying to *understand* how he or she feels. This is where active listening comes in. Actively listening to the other person helps them feel understood and encourages them to say more.

Although active listening is a simple process, it requires a positive, engaged attitude and plenty of practice! It's all about what you say in words and involves such things as utterances, paraphrasing and clarifying.

Utterances

Utterances include small verbal comments like 'yes', and 'uh huh', 'go on' or 'I see'. You are conveying your interest and encouraging the other person to continue talking.

Reflecting, paraphrasing

This involves reflecting back and summarising what the other person has said, to confirm your understanding. Typically, you would use words and phrases like 'So, as I understand it...' and 'What I think you're saying is...am I right?' and 'Okay, you think that...?' or 'You feel that...?'

Reflecting back what the other person said is not easy; while the other person is speaking, you, the listener have to keep in mind the main points and details about what the other person is communicating.

Once again, you do not have to agree with how the other person feels; you only need to convey what you've understood about how they're feeling. If it appears to the other person that you have *not* understood, he or she can explain some more.

Of course, it would be quite unnatural to repeat or paraphrase what you have heard every time someone spoke to you!

The trick is to listen *as if* you were going to reflect and paraphrase (whether you do so or not). This is why reflective listening is so powerful. It focuses your attention, helps you to listen, helps the other person to feel understood and encourages further communication.

brilliant example

Active listening

Rebecca	I am so embarrassed. I forgot to bring some information that Jack needed at the meeting yesterday.
Sally	Really? (Utterance)
Rebecca	Yes. And now he's avoiding me. Today, Chris, who sits opposite me, told me Jack had been complaining to the rest of the office that I'm so disorganised.
Sally	Hmmm, so the whole office heard Jack complaining about you. (Paraphrasing)

Rebecca	Yes.
Sally	How do you feel about that?
Rebecca	I'm quite upset. I really want to clear the air – I've tried to apologise but he is giving me the silent treatment. Actually, I'm getting angry about it now.
Sally	Let me get this right. You were embarrassed and upset that you forgot something so important, but now you're getting angry with Jack because he's not giving you the chance to apologise. (Reflecting, paraphrasing and clarifying)
Rebecca	Yes. That's exactly right.
Sally	What's the next step? (Open question)
Rebecca	Maybe I'll email him. Say I'm sorry and explain what I can do to make sure I don't forget to bring any information he needs to future meetings.
Sally	Sounds good to me.

brilliant example

You'll often find that you can interpret what someone has said just in terms of feelings. Imagine, for example, that a friend told you how a colleague of his was praised for a piece of work she had successfully completed. Your friend's contribution however was not acknowledged. You say, 'It sounds like you felt *disappointed*.' He will either agree or clarify by replying, for example, 'Actually I was more than disappointed really; I was quite upset.'

exercise 5 Practise active listening with a friend

One of you talks for two minutes on one of the subjects, below. The other person must use active listening techniques to show interest and understanding. Most importantly, when the speaker has finished speaking, the listener must reflect back what he or she thinks the speaker *felt; their emotions.* Show acceptance and understanding of his or her feelings.

● A time when you received poor service in a shop, restaurant or bank.

● The best job or holiday you ever had.

● The worst job or holiday you ever had.

● Your opinion about the death penalty.

Active listening is a powerful technique that will enable you to develop your emotional intelligence in the following ways:

Develop empathy and rapport

By trying to understand what the other person is saying and feeling, you show that you *are* trying to see things from their point of view.

Overcome your assumptions

Your assumptions, your beliefs and your own emotions can distort what you hear. Active listening techniques deter you from 'jumping in' and assuming you know how another person feels. And, with active listening, the other person can confirm or refute your perception and interpretation of what they've said and how they feel.

Encourage him or her to open up

Because you don't interrupt and break the flow of the other person's thoughts and feelings with your own opinion, unnecessary questions or comment, when you do reflect back what the other person said and they confirm, retract or adjust what they feel, it can also encourage the speaker to open up, and say more.

Gives you control in difficult situations

Reflecting back slows everything down. This gives both sides time to think about how they feel.

What happens if you can't listen? If you are too busy, distracted, confused or worried to focus on what the other person is saying? Say so! Don't be afraid to tell the other person that you can't listen right now. Rather than risk the other person feeling rushed into explaining what's happened and how they feel or the other person feeling that you aren't interested, explain

> don't be afraid to tell the other person that you can't listen right now

why this isn't a good time for you. Unless what they have to say is urgent, negotiate a time when you will be more able to give your full attention. And keep to it.

brilliant example

Moira had a report to complete and she was getting close to the deadline when Jamie approached her and began telling her his plans for a project they were going to be working on the following month. 'Jamie, I'm sorry', said Moria, 'but I can't listen to your ideas right now. I'm up against a deadline and feeling quite stressed about it. I'll be free after lunch. Can we meet up to talk then and I can give you my full attention. I'm keen to hear your ideas!'

Facilitative listening

Facilitative listening is the next step in developing rapport, understanding and empathy. Facilitative listening is concerned with being interested in helping the other person to express themselves. It involves asking questions and clarifying.

Clarifying – asking open questions

Even when you've done your best to accept and acknowledge what the other person has said you still might not be clear about what he or she is saying or feels.

A simple way to clarify or get more information is to ask the type of questions that encourage the other person to express their thoughts and feelings. Asking 'open' questions does this. Open questions usually begin with what, why, how, tell me, explain and describe. For example, 'How did that happen?', and 'Can you tell me when...?', and 'What did you mean by...?', 'Why do you think he said that?', and 'Tell me how you feel about that.'

Open questions can be asked as and whenever you need to clarify a point or find out more, at different points in a conversation. Closed questions, such as 'Are you OK?' and 'Do you know how to do it?', on the other hand, can be answered with a single word – usually yes or no. Closed questions keep control with the questioner, whereas open questions give the other person the opportunity to say more.

brilliant tip

How often do you ask people about their feelings with 'yes' or 'no' questions? For example, 'Are you ok with this?', 'Are you upset?', 'Are you happy now?' These all or nothing questions mean that the other person really only has two possible responses: 'yes' or 'no'.

One way to help someone better convey how they are feeling is to suggest they measure their feelings from 0–10. For example, 'How disappointed are you, from 0 to 10?'

Most people will simply ask, 'Are you disappointed?' But what will a yes or no answer really tell you? Not a great deal. Try asking 'How disappointed are you - on a scale of 1–10?' Asking the question this way gives you both an insight into the extent of their feelings and from that you can ask further questions. For example, 'Oh, you'd rate your disappointment with a 10! It's been quite a crushing blow for you, then. Is there anything I can do to help you feel a bit better?

Funnel questions

Open questions can also be used in a technique known as 'funnel questioning'. Funnel questions are a series of questions that seek further information that either goes into more detail or becomes more general.

Funnel questions that increase detail gives you, the listener, more information about fewer topics and helps the other person to focus and recall detail. You start with general questions, and then narrow in on an issue in each answer, getting more detail with each question.

For example:

> *Ed*   *Tell me more* about the problem between you.
>
> *Jamila*   Lewis and I had an argument and we haven't spoken since.
>
> *Ed*   What, *specifically*, was it about?
>
> *Jamila*   We're getting behind on a deadline for a project and he thinks that because I work part time I can't

possibly understand what it is like to have to take on extra work. I have other commitments too you know.

Ed   How, *exactly* do you feel about that?

Jamila   Angry with him and embarrassed for myself – we rowed in front of the rest of the office.

An advantage of the funnel questioning technique is that it can be used to defuse conflict or a difficult situation and help the other person calm down and feel understood. Funnel questions get the other person to go into more detail about their prob-

lem. This can help the other person

> funnel questions get the other person to go into more detail about their problem

to disengage from their emotions and help both of you to clarify and understand the situation. Beginning by saying 'Tell me more about what happened...' is a general invitation that gets the other person started and gives you, the listener, the opportunity to pick up on and ask further questions about the specific details.

Using words like 'specifically', 'exactly' or 'in particular' in your questions directs the other person to explain a particular point, in more detail. Use these words along with 'How?' and 'What?'.

Funnel questions that *increase* detail give you, the listener, more information about fewer topics. On the other hand, funnel questions that *decrease* the need for detail broaden out the questions to give you wider information about more general topics. Such questions begin, for example, with: 'Who else?' and 'What else?'.

'So, he accepted your apology. Then what happened? *What else* did you discuss?'

This way of questioning can be useful in situations where you want to encourage the person you're speaking with to open up.

brilliant tip

Make sure that you give the person you're questioning enough time to respond. They may need to think before they answer, so don't interpret a pause as an opportunity for you to take over the conversation.

brilliant example

If you're not sure, if you are not entirely clear about the other person's situation, do ask questions. Listen to news programmes on the radio and TV. Note how often Sarah Montague on Radio 4's *Today* programme, Jeremy Vine on Radio 2 and Kirsty Wark on BBC 2's *Newsnight* ask questions to clarify both their own and the listeners' understanding.

Nonverbal communication

Developing empathy and being open to other people's perspectives requires effort on your part. Other people don't always spell out what they really think or what they're feeling. They do, however, give clues. Look for these clues. You have plenty to help you; not just what he or she says, but how they say it, their body language, their actions and how they respond to what you say. Practise by being more aware of the connections between verbal and nonverbal communication. Do they all 'say' the same thing? Also, watch out for changes in the way the other person communicates.

Be aware of your own nonverbal communication when you are asking questions. Be sure that your questions don't come across as interrogative, attacking, defensive or rude. Your facial expressions, gestures and tone of voice all play a part in the answers you get when you ask questions.

Talking to other people: the other person's perspective

Your main aim when you're talking to other people? To make it easy for them to understand you. Just because you've explained or described something, don't assume that the other person will understand what you mean or feel the same way as you. Consider *their* situation. What do they already know about what you are telling them? What might their feelings and beliefs be? Do you even know if this is a good time and place for them to listen to what you have to say?

Managing other people's feelings and emotions isn't just about listening to them and knowing how to respond. It also means knowing *when* to talk about something. That's emotionally intelligent! Often, there really is a good and bad time to talk about things; there are times when others are more open and receptive to listening and talking. If you're not sure, just ask; 'Is this a good time to talk about...?

brilliant example

George and Etta have been married for six years. During the week, George is at home looking after their two young sons while Etta works at a hospice. For George, Etta's arrival home from work, was often the first opportunity he'd had to talk to another adult all day. But Etta needed time to disengage from work and spend time with the children. George has learnt that the best time to talk about anything with his wife is not in the first hour of her returning home each day. Etta is far more receptive after she's bathed the children, put them to bed and she and George are having a meal together.

As well as knowing when others are going to be most receptive to listening and talking, be aware when the other person needs a break. If the conversation becomes too heated, if he or she is confused, upset, tired or needs time to reflect, do suggest that can you resume the conversation later.

Ask questions

Sometimes you can tell if the other person isn't engaging with what you're saying – not because they've told you, but from their nonverbal communication – a look of confusion on their face, for example. Other times, you can't be certain. Instead of rattling on, pause occasionally and ask 'What do *you* think?' or 'How do *you* feel about that?'

If they look at you blankly, repeat the question and add what you were talking about; '*What do you think* about the idea of making organ donor cards mandatory?' or 'I've been worried about Mum since she came home from hospital. *How do you feel* about her situation?'

 When you ask a person to tell you how they feel, the very act of thinking about a feeling changes the feeling.

A.K. Pradeep, Observer, 15 January 2012

brilliant tip

Ask questions in terms of thoughts *and* feelings. For example, ask 'What do you *think* about that?' Then ask 'And how do you *feel* about that?'

There is a difference in asking different people how they feel over what they think. Remember, emotions are made up of both thoughts and feelings. There are often times when it can help you and the

▶

other person if you ask questions in terms of thoughts *and* feelings. For example,

You   What do you *think* about Mum going into a home?

Your brother I think it's the only practical solution. Mum can't look after herself anymore.

You   How do you *feel* about that?

Your brother Sad. Sad that Mum has to leave our family home. On the other hand, if she's in a home nearer to me I'll feel happier; I'll feel reassured that she's safe and I can visit her more often.

brilliant recap

- The emotionally intelligent approach to managing other people's emotions involves having empathy.

- Empathy means being willing to try and understand and respond to someone else's situation, their point of view, their thoughts and feelings.

- Empathy starts with listening to the other person – listening to not just what he or she says, but also what they don't say – their nonverbal language.

- Listening involves accepting and acknowledging what the other person is saying and feeling.

- Facilitative listening is concerned with being interested in helping the other person to express themselves. It involves asking questions and clarifying.

- Managing other people's feelings and emotions isn't just about listening to them. It also means knowing when and how to respond.

PART 2

Manage
emotions

CHAPTER 8

Persuade and influence

W hether you are hoping to persuade your partner to clean the loo, your teenage son to join you on holiday or persuade colleagues to change their approach to a project, there are several key emotional intelligence principles you must follow.

⬤⬤⬤ **brilliant** example

Marcella is a member of a residents' community group. The local church are selling the Victorian church hall and the group are hoping to buy the hall for the community by offering residents the opportunity to buy shares. Marcella is not convinced that this is going to be the best approach - will enough residents buy shares? And will more money have to be found to renovate the hall? It's occurred to Marcella that there might be a more effective way to buy the hall. But, she has to persuade the rest of the group!

Where to start? There are several steps to take if you want to win people over to your way of thinking.

1. Be clear about your message. Make sure you know what, exactly it is that you want to persuade the other person to do. Distinguish between *needs* – important points on which you can't compromise – and *interests* – issues where you can con-

cede ground. What about your feelings? Do you need to explain how you feel about the issue? Persuasion requires and involves emotion, but don't let feelings take over. Simplify the message and don't ramble on. People who successfully persuade others make it easy for them to understand.

2. Ask yourself what you already know about the other person or people that might help you to engage them. How might they feel about the issue or situation? What are their interests and goals? Marcella's neighbours' goal is to secure the hall for continued community use. Marcella drew on this goal to suggest that securing a space for community use might not have to mean keeping the old hall.

3. Choose a good time so you can *persuade* the other person when he or she is at their most responsive. Marcella knew that a discussion about the extent of renovation costs was on the agenda. She waited till then to make her point.

4. Accentuate the positive. When you are trying to persuade someone to do something, tell them how it will benefit them. It's important to be genuine and sincere. Don't behave as if you are superior or have superior knowledge. A good attitude will certainly help; people will listen to what you have to say without thinking that you want to force your point of view on them. Marcella admitted she had no idea what a new build would cost; she suggested they get some professional advice from an architect about rebuilding costs.

5. Certainly point out what you think the consequences will be of not doing things the way you want, but don't use emotional blackmail, threats or punishments that the other person will incur if they don't do things your way!

6. Use empathy. Anticipate objections and concerns and address them – you can do this by putting yourself in the other person's place and imagining what their objections might be.

Marcella imagined that some people would argue that the building was of historical importance and should be saved (although it wasn't listed). She was prepared for this and ready to point out that the hall was so old that it may cost too much to renovate. This would mean that no one would buy it and it could fall into a state of total disrepair. She also pointed out that the hall was built for the needs of people 150 years ago. 'We need a hall to meet twenty-first-century community needs,' she said.

Be a good listener and take the other person's point of view into consideration. People are far more willing to cooperate if they feel acknowledged, understood and appreciated.

7. Negotiate. Know when to compromise.

8. Ask questions. What incentives does the other person need? Use reasoning to discuss ways to overcome any barriers.

9. Use positive, rather than negative language: instead of saying 'You're wrong about this', say 'I understand that you think/feel that, but...', or 'I agree with what you say on ... but have you considered ...'.

10. Listen not just to what is being said, but to what is not being said and be aware of your own nonverbal communication. Use open, encouraging body language not defensive or closed.

11. Acknowledge but don't make a big deal about any gain you stand to receive should the other person choose your preferred course of action.

12. Know when to cut your losses and give up trying to persuade. Plan for alternative outcomes if you can't reach agreement.

People who are convinced against their will, are of the same opinion still.

Samuel Butler

Know what you want but keep in mind that persuasion should use suggestion not demand. Certainly, you can get people to do what you want by making demands or being manipulative but that's not persuasion, forcing people to achieve things in a way that works for *you* and probably only serves *your* interests. You might succeed in getting things done in the short term, but you won't succeed in winning support in the long run.

brilliant recap

- Be clear and specific; make sure you know what, exactly, it is that you want to persuade the other person to do.

- Think about what you already know about the other person; how might they feel about the issue or situation?

- Choose a good time so you can persuade the other person when he or she is at their most responsive.

- Be positive. Don't patronise or use threats or put-downs.

- Be a good listener. Address objections and concerns.

- Be prepared to negotiate and compromise.

- Be aware of nonverbal communication.

- Know when to give up; plan for alternative outcomes if you can't reach agreement.

CHAPTER 9

Delegate

There are only 24 hours in a day. There's only so much you can achieve in those hours however hard you work. Whether at work or home, trying to do everything can leave you stressed, overloaded and disappointed. This is why delegation is such an important skill. There is no shame in handing over to someone else, so swallow your pride and show respect for the skills, knowledge and experience that others can contribute.

brilliant example

Greg has his own immigration consultancy business. He had an urgent case to work on but was snowed under and needed some help. Greg asked Jenna to make some phone calls to get some information for him. 'Yeah sure', said Jenna, without looking up from a series of spreadsheets she was working on.

When he checked with her in the afternoon Jenna - with a cold stare - told Greg that she'd forgotten to make the calls. Greg pressed Jenna to drop everything and do what he needed straight away. Jenna made the calls but she didn't get all the information that Greg needed and he ended up having to follow up two of the phone calls himself.

What went wrong? Like many people, for Greg, what passes for delegation, for the other person, feels like dumping. To Jenna, it seemed that Greg wasn't coping and so he just off loaded work onto her - tasks that she wasn't especially efficient at and at a time when she also had a lot to do.

Time to stop dumping in the name of delegation!

Unsuccessful attempts at delegation in the past can often leave you feeling that it's more trouble than it's worth. Next time, you tell yourself, it will be easier and quicker to do it yourself than explain it to someone else. Not true! With a bit of time and effort, you *can* get things done through other people.

Choose the right task for the right person

The best person to delegate a task to will be the person with the relevant experience, knowledge and skills. Unless you've got plenty of time to show someone or train them to do something that is unfamiliar to them, choose a task that matches a person's skills and ability.

Greg hadn't considered whether making phone calls was not a good use of Jenna's time and skills. It hadn't occurred to Greg that she might feel resentful.

What Jenna *is* very good at, is inputting information onto spreadsheets. Next time he needed to delegate, rather than ask Jenna to make phone calls, Greg got the information he needed and then asked Jenna to use her skills to create a spreadsheet for him. Because she was asked to do what she was good at, Jenna was happy to help out.

You will also need to consider the other person's current workload; does he or she actually have time to take on more work? Will you delegating this task require reshuffling of other commitments? If so, what do they think and how do they feel about that? What are their concerns? Ask them. Include people in the delegation process. Empower them to decide what tasks are to be delegated to them and when.

Clearly identify what needs doing

People who successfully delegate are clear about what they want. They make it easy for others to understand what needs doing, how and by when. Begin with the end in mind and explain the desired results. Tell the other person what you want and then listen to the response. Be aware of their nonverbal communication – what's that telling you about how they feel?

Greg learnt that the most effective way to be clear about a task was to say what he needed first, then offer to write it in an email, so Jenna could check what Greg needed doing.

Motivate the other person

State the benefit; explain what's in it for the other person and deliver it as the most attractive possibility. For example, Greg saying to Jenna 'I need you to do this for me', is likely to mean a lot less than 'If you could do this, I'll be able to get this completed today and the client will give us more cases in future. That will keep us both in work!'

It's important to be positive and sincere – no emotional blackmail! Do not manipulate people with low level threats of how badly either you or they will feel if they don't cooperate!

Follow-up

At some point, see if the person is ok and needs any further support or resources. Be available to answer questions but don't micro manage; focus on the end result rather than detailing exactly how the work should be done. Your way is not necessarily the only or even the best way! Let people do things their own way; this creates trust.

> let people do things their own way; this creates trust

Make sure you express your appreciation; the other person will know that their efforts have been acknowledged and they will be more likely to help out next time.

To delegate effectively, choose the right tasks to delegate, to the right person, and delegate in the right way. You will increase what gets done, make the best use of yours and other people's time and skills and reduce your own workload and stress. That's emotionally intelligent!

brilliant recap

- Choose the right task for the right person.
- Make it easy for others to understand what needs doing, how and by when.
- Motivate the other person; provide an incentive.
- Provide support if and when necessary.

CHAPTER 10

Cut your losses

We must accept finite disappointment but never lose finite hope.

Martin Luther King

Imagine you have an old friend who every time you see her or talk on the phone, you find you have less and less in common with her; you have less to talk about. Since her divorce five years ago she's become more and more bitter and resentful. Her negative attitude simply drains you. Would you continue to keep in touch or quietly let the friendship fade away?

Or, suppose you've been following a particular career path for several months, and you're increasingly feeling that it's 'not you'. Do you go back to your last job (it's available) and work on a new project or stick with the more prestigious and better paid job you're in now?

Or, what if you signed up for a course of exercise classes. After two classes you realise you've made a mistake. You hate going! Do you continue to drag yourself to the gym each week?

Whatever it is and whether this realisation comes after a month, a year, or half a lifetime, why, despite your disappointment or unhappiness might you find it difficult to cut your losses and move on?

One of the main reasons many of us find it difficult to call it a day is because we're thinking about what we've got to lose; the time, effort, love or money we have already put in and that we can't get back.

These 'sunk costs' can fool us into sticking with something we would be best off ending, so we continue to put more time, effort or money into someone or something even though it's plainly not doing us any good.

It's an emotionally intelligent person who realises that their efforts are getting them nowhere. Here's how to cut your losses and move on:

Identify how you feel

Feelings of regret? Disappointed with how things have turned out? Don't carry on making yourself miserable just because you think that all that past misery would be wasted otherwise! Reason must be part of doing things, but not the only part of it. Instead, use your feelings wisely to inform what you do next.

Focus on the positive

The best and easiest way to cut your losses and move on is to identify and focus on what you have to *gain* rather than what you have to lose by pulling out.

Of course, letting go of an old friendship, for example, will be sad. But focus on how relieved you will feel, that no longer seeing her will mean you will have more time to spend with more positive friends.

In many cases it's true that you shouldn't give up too early; sometimes you know you need to push past temporary difficulties or discomfort in order to get where you want to be. But if the bad feelings persist, take notice!

Yes, you will feel embarrassed to admit that the new job didn't turn out as you'd hoped, but think of the joy you'll feel at being back doing a job you enjoy with people you like on a new, interesting project and, suddenly, it's a whole lot easier to let go.

And yes, you may have spent that money up front on classes – but if you stop going and instead do an exercise like cycling or walking that's free and you know you will enjoy, you're quids in! And, you're now finally *convinced* that you're never going to enjoy any sort of exercise class no matter how often your friends recommend it.

If you identify and then focus on the good things that could happen by pulling out, not only will you find it easier to accept what you have already lost, you'll see new opportunities and feel confident you are making the right decision.

Know that you made the right choice in the past

No matter how long you've put up with something, you can always draw something good out. At the very least, you'll have learnt something about yourself. Maybe your friendship gave you lots of travel adventures together when you were young, free and single? Great! Nothing can change that.

Whatever it is that you're holding on to, ask yourself why – is it because you really will gain something at the end or because you don't want to lose the time, energy or money you've already invested? If it's the latter, focus on what you have to gain and move forward!

brilliant recap

- Too much thinking about what you've got to lose, can fool you into sticking with something you'd be best off ending.
- Know that you made the right choice in the past.
- Focus on what you have to *gain* rather than what you have to lose by pulling out.

CHAPTER 11

When you don't like someone

D o you have to deal with people you don't like? Someone at work maybe or someone in the family who rubs you up the wrong way? Do you struggle to manage your feelings and remain civil? Good news! It *can* be done!

brilliant example

Although Dionne was looking forward to her mother's seventieth birthday party that evening, she was anxious about seeing her brother-in-law Ross. He often seemed to enjoy humiliating her. Last month, for example, at a family lunch, Ross contradicted Dionne's views and opinions. And last week, on the phone, Ross dismissed Dionne's idea for a present for her mother.

If Dionne gets upset at his remarks, Ross just laughs it off or claims that she is over sensitive. (This is typical passive aggressive behaviour; the other person – Ross – finds a way to blame someone else and shirk the responsibility for his behaviour. It is underhand, manipulative and unkind behaviour.) Although Dionne really dislikes Ross, she hesitates to stand up to him; she's worried that if she did, she'd lose control, completely freak out at him and upset the rest of the family.

In a situation like this it's easy to feel powerless. You may think you just have to put up with people who behave like that, but, instead of worrying about how much fear and anxiety you feel, focus on dealing with other person *despite* your fears or worries.

brilliant tip

Before you say anything, check your body language. Remember, how you sit or stand actually affects the way your brain functions. Carry yourself with confidence and in a matter of minutes your body will start to feel it and your brain will start to believe it.

Even when you are feeling intimidated or self-conscious you can convey feelings that you're not actually experiencing; you can positively influence how you feel by simply changing your posture. It's up to you to make sure your brain is getting the right message. If you want to feel more in control and confident, not just *appear* confident, but genuinely feel confident, simply choose to do just two or three of these actions:

- stand or sit straight;
- keep your head level;
- relax your shoulders;
- spread your weight evenly on both legs;
- if sitting, keep your elbows on the arms of your chair (rather than tightly against your sides);
- make appropriate eye contact;
- lower the pitch of your voice;
- speak more slowly.

If you can do one or two of those things consistently, your thoughts, feelings and the rest of your nonverbal signals will catch up. It's a dynamic process where small changes in how you use your body can add up to a big change in how you feel, how you behave and the impact you have on other people.

A good way to start is to say, 'Could you say that again – I'm not sure what you mean'. This is useful as it turns the attention on the other person and their intentions and gives you a bit more time to collect yourself.

Decide how their comments have made you feel. Embarrassed? Humiliated? Frustrated? Hurt or anxious?

Once you know how you feel, you can let the other person know. Start by saying '*I* feel' and not '*you* are making me feel'. Saying, for example, '*You* are making me embarrassed',

> once you know how you feel, you can let the other person know

blames the other person for how you feel. On the other hand, saying, '*I* am feeling embarrassed by what you said', is taking responsibility for feeling that way. And no one can argue with that – they can't say 'no you don't'.

Resist the urge to back down, argue or sulk. Simply look them in the eye and leave it at that.

For example, at Dionne's mother's birthday party Ross *did* make a barbed comment. 'Oh Dionne what a shame you and Steve divorced last year – I'm sorry you're on your own for your Mum's birthday – I wonder if she's disappointed.'

Dionne shifted her posture so that she was standing straight. She made eye contact and smiled. 'I'm not sure I understand what you're saying. Could you tell me what you mean?' 'Oh come on, you know what I'm getting at', said Ross.

'No', said Dionne, 'I don't know what you mean. In fact I feel confused and a little embarrassed.' She then held his gaze, smiled and said, 'Anyway, I have to go and speak to my brother. See you later.'

The result? Dionne has confronted both her fears and the other person (Ross). She has also managed to say how she felt. She remained civil and in control of the situation.

While it is not always possible to cut out people from your life whom you dislike, you can at least try not to let them have emotional power over you. Judge the success of your interactions with others by how well you have behaved. Even if the other person does not change, you can walk away knowing that you have behaved assertively. That's emotionally intelligent!

brilliant recap

- Instead of thinking about how much fear and anxiety you feel, focus your thoughts on dealing with the other person *despite* your fears or worries.

- No need to argue, blame, shrivel or sulk. Simply stand or sit straight, make eye contact and let the other person know how you feel.

- Take control, change the subject and move onto something (or someone) else.

CHAPTER 12

When you are angry

Anyone can become angry –
that's easy, but to be angry with
the right person at the right time,
and for the right purpose and in
the right way – that is not within
everyone's power and that is not
easy.

Aristotle

The anger has kept me going.
Without it I'll crumble.

Doreen Lawrence – mother of
Stephen Lawrence

s it wrong to feel angry? No. Anger is a normal human emotion; it's a natural response to feeling wronged, offended threatened or attacked in some way. Of course, no one likes to be on the receiving end or witness anger, though, because anger can be frightening and lead to destructive and violent behaviour.

That's because when something makes you feel angry, tension builds up. It's released when you express your anger. As long as the build-up of tension is released in actions or words that are relatively safe, the release is a positive thing; helping to keep body and mind in balance. But, if you *suppress* your anger, the energy from all that tension may turn inwards and have negative physical and psychological effects.

brilliant recap

Behaviour and beliefs about anger

Many of us have been brought up to believe that anger is 'bad' or 'wrong'.

Maybe you were reprimanded, even punished for expressing anger and frustration when you were small. Or you may have been frightened by the strength of your own bad temper. Perhaps you've learnt to suppress and deny feelings of anger?

On the other hand, if you were brought up in a family where you learnt that expressing your anger is normal, it may seem to other people that you can't control your anger.

My friend Cindy once told me 'In our family, no one ever shouts or throws things. Sometimes, I wish that they would. They just make snide comments, or sulk, or refuse to talk to each other for weeks.'

How did your family manage anger? Who got angry, and what happened when they did? If no one showed their anger, what happened with resentments and disagreements?

How do past beliefs about anger affect you now? Do you still believe them? How do you behave when you're angry? Do you tend to bottle things up, or do you tend to explode?

If you would like to deal with angry feelings better, try the following advice.

Take time out

If your anger is at a rage stage, you need to release some of it. This will reduce the possibility of losing control and also increase your ability to think more clearly. So, when you feel yourself getting angry, stop and ask yourself, 'Am I so angry I can't think clearly or so angry I want to lash out, verbally or physically?'

If the answer is yes and someone else is involved tell him or her that you are too angry to talk at the moment. But whether your anger is directed at someone else or not, take some time out; go for a walk. If you want, let out the need to lash out by hitting a cushion, breaking crockery and/or crying, shouting, screaming or swearing where it will not alarm anyone.

> whether your anger is directed at someone else or not, take some time out

brilliant tip

Breathe

Remember, anger has very obvious physical aspects; increased heart rate, breathing and muscle tension. Slowing down your breathing can help slow your heart rate back to a normal level and help calm you back down. So, stop breathing for five seconds (to 'reset' your breath) then breathe in slowly for three seconds, then breathe out *even more slowly*. Keep doing this and remember it's the *out-breath* that will slow everything down.

Think

Even when you're angry, if you really need to, you *can* still engage the thinking part of your brain. You can do this by simply forcing yourself to recite the alphabet in your head, counting backwards from 20 or even remembering everything you had to eat and drink yesterday. Try it; it really will work.

Be assertive

Once you feel capable of thinking clearly, you can think through what you want to say and what you want to happen. Expressing your angry feelings in an assertive – not aggressive or passive aggressive – manner is the emotionally intelligent way to manage the problem.

An assertive approach includes:

- Taking responsibility and not blaming the other person for how you feel.
- Telling the other person clearly and succinctly how you feel and why. Not waffling or ranting!
- Listening and being open to the other person's response.

- Setting boundaries and limits; what you will and will not accept.

- Knowing when to compromise and negotiate and when to stand your ground and insist.

- Being prepared to take the consequences of communicating your feelings.

brilliant example

Joe and Martin had been friends since university ten years ago. Martin came to visit Joe for the weekend. On the Saturday evening they went for dinner at the village pub. Martin got drunk and made a huge fuss about his meal not being what he had expected. He was offensive and insulting, first, to the waitress and then to the owner of the pub, who was a friend of Joe's. Joe was very angry with Martin for his behaviour.

As they left the pub. Martin started making excuses for his performance but Joe said he couldn't talk about it now and when they returned home Joe said he was off to bed.

The next morning, Joe thought about how he felt and what he wanted and spoke to Martin. Sitting opposite Martin at the kitchen table, he said, 'Martin, I feel angry about the way you spoke to the people at the pub last night. It was rude and offensive. I'm upset that the evening ended badly.' Martin said he was sorry but he'd got drunk and didn't mean to be rude and that he didn't think he'd made that big a deal. 'And anyway', said Martin, 'The food and service *was* poor.' Joe listened to Martin. He acknowledged what Martin said but stood his ground; 'Yes, the food and service weren't brilliant. But, you might not think you were rude, but I do. I'd like it if you apologised to the people at the pub.'

Watch for early signs of anger. Only you know the danger signs when your anger is building, so learn to recognise them when they begin.

Choose your time. Talk to the other person when he or she is unlikely to be distracted and more likely to listen to you. Be somewhere that allows you to feel that you are both equal and that you both matter. Either sit in chairs at the same height, or both stand up.

Explain how you feel. Once you have thought about what you want to say, talk to the other person sooner rather than later. Don't think for so long that your anger builds up.

Be specific. Say, 'I feel angry with you because...' This avoids blaming the other person, and shows that you are taking responsibility for how you feel. The other person is then less likely to feel attacked.

Listen to the other person's response, and try to understand their point of view. Treat them with the same attention and respect that you want from them.

Set boundaries and limits. Explain what you want to happen next and what you will and will not accept in the future.

In Joe and Martin's case, if Martin had agreed to apologise to the people at the pub, Joe might simply have thanked Martin and decided that in future, when Martin visited, he wouldn't go out to a pub or restaurant with him again.

But if Martin had refused to apologise Joe might decide to compromise and say to Martin 'OK, as long as you promise not to behave like that again when we go out.' But if Joe decided he was going to stand his ground, he'd also need to decide what would happen if Martin didn't do what he asked. Not invite him down again, for example, or see Martin less often?

Use anger to put an end to the problems not your relationships. When something needs to change, anger not only lets you know but it can give you the power to do something about it.

Of course, you won't always get the opportunity to express your anger to the other person. Like most people, you've probably found yourself fuming at someone else's bad driving. It's certainly not advisable to drive after the other driver and confront him or her. So what can you do?

Again, take responsibility for how you feel. '*I'm* furious' rather than 'Her bad driving made me furious.'

You might not be able to tell the other person how you feel but you *can* calm down inside. This means managing your internal responses, taking steps to lower your heart rate, calm yourself down, and let the feelings subside. There's more than one way to do this – you have a choice.

If you're too angry to drive, pull over somewhere safe and shout, scream or swear; pull over to a shop or café and buy a drink; or take a short walk. Phone a friend and tell them what happened and how angry you are. Listen to music. Put on some heavy rock music and sing at the top of your voice to help you release your anger. Play something slow and mellow to help you calm down.

Reframe the situation. If, instead of being real life it had been a computer driving game, would the same incident have enraged you or would you have seen it as a challenge in the game to skilfully negotiate? Congratulate yourself on having avoided a nasty incident!

Dealing with anger in other people

As well as being a response to feeling wronged, offended, threatened or attacked in some way, anger happens when the expectations and beliefs a person has about a situation and the way things 'should' be, differ to what actually happens. The person sees that difference as a *negative* thing. For example, Joe *expected* Martin to behave in a civil manner. When Martin behaved in a way Joe didn't expect and didn't like, Joe got angry. People who suffer with road rage assume that everyone else will drive with due care and attention. They are enraged when that doesn't happen! Are their expectations unrealistic?

> the key to managing someone else's anger is to start by understanding their expectations

The key to managing someone else's anger is to start by understanding what their expectations were. To do this, you'll need to use your listening skills and take an assertive approach.

Accept the other person's feelings

When a person is feeling angry, it's easy for him or her to become irrational and illogical because the anger has overwhelmed their rational mind. So, if you're faced with an angry person, it's as if you are communicating with the emotion, not the person; a wall has come down.

If at any point, the other person is so angry that they are confusing or scaring you, suggest time out. Say, 'I know you're furious about what happened but I'm feeling confused or scared. Let's take ten minutes and then talk about it.'

Listen first, ask questions later

An angry person wants to vent their feelings so don't say anything until they have finished their outburst. Acknowledge what they are saying without interrupting to defend yourself or disagree because the moment that you oppose what they are saying you're adding fuel to the fire.

Check your body language; it won't be easy, but try and focus on a couple of things that will help keep you feeling in control.

- stand or sit straight;
- keep your head level;
- relax your shoulders;
- spread your weight evenly on both legs.

When you *do* respond, lower the pitch of your voice and speak more slowly. Start by repeating back some of the main points or comments that have been made such as: 'Ok, you're saying that you don't like it when...' Then, ask the other person what they want to happen next. For example, 'What do you want me to do?' or 'What would you like to do about it?'

Then, state how *you* feel and how *you* see the situation. You might disagree with their perspective and what they expect. But, you may agree with their point of view and, if their anger is directed at you, apologise and explain what you can do to rectify the situation.

Either way, by using listening skills you show that you're taking the other person seriously and you slow the situation down. And, to learn to deal with it in other people is to learn to manage it within ourselves.

brilliant recap

- Only you know when your anger is building, so watch for early signs.
- Take time out. Give yourself time to think more clearly, but don't think for so long that your anger builds up.
- Calm down inside. Take steps to lower your heart rate, calm yourself down and let strong feelings subside.
- Think. Even when you're angry, if you really need to, you *can* still engage the thinking part of your brain.

- Reframe the situation. Is there another, more helpful way to think about the problem?

- Express your anger in an assertive way; be specific about why you are angry, what you do and don't want to happen. Listen to the other person's response and give them the same respect that you want from them.

- If you're faced with an angry person, know that it's easy for him or her to become irrational and illogical because the anger has overwhelmed their rational mind.

- Listen first, ask questions later.

- If the other person is so angry that they are confusing or scaring you, suggest time out.

- When you do respond, lower the pitch of your voice and speak more slowly.

CHAPTER 13

The power of
the positive

Giving compliments and appreciation

Giving compliments and praise, expressing appreciation and gratitude are emotionally intelligent things to do. How come? Well, not only do your comments let the other person know that their actions and efforts have been noticed, but also other people feel good if they know they've helped to make you feel good!

Don't let worry about getting the wording right stop you from saying something; just know that a genuine sentiment phrased a bit awkwardly is better than no appreciation being showed at all. And anyway, your body language, tone of voice and facial expressions will show that your compliment or appreciation is genuine.

> a genuine sentiment phrased a bit awkwardly is better than no appreciation being showed at all

To help you, follow the steps below.

Give a clear reason why you are complimenting or praising the other person

The most appreciated compliment is often the most specific one, because it shows that you really did notice. For example:

'I wanted to say thanks for being such a supportive tutor.'

'I wanted to say well done on your success at being awarded the grant.'

Acknowledge personal qualities or special efforts

For example:

> 'You have a way of explaining difficult concepts.'

> 'You clearly have a talent for writing funding bids.'

Explain how their actions have made you feel

People feel good if they know they've made you feel good. So, if what they have done has had a positive effect on you, tell them!

Put your emotions into words. Words like grateful, excited, surprised, happy, pleasant, calm, thrilled, tickled pink, pleased, thankful, reassured, overjoyed and glad, all help convey appreciation.

> 'Thanks to you, I feel more confident about my ability to write academic essays. I'm so pleased.'

> 'I feel relieved and much more optimistic that we can raise the necessary funds.'

When you tell the other person that they have made a positive difference, he or she can then feel good about themselves and encouraged because of the positive impact their actions had on how you feel.

Express appreciation

> 'Thanks.'

> 'I'm very grateful.'

Be aware though, that for some people and in some cultures, it is polite to deny compliments and a person may refuse a compliment for this reason. Don't press the point – in this case, the appropriate response from you is a smile.

Go the extra mile: put it in writing

When it's appropriate send a letter, card or email expressing your appreciation. This shows effort on your part while also giving the person a permanent reminder of the praise.

brilliant tip

Reward publicly, admonish privately.

Accepting compliments and praise

Some people are uncomfortable with accepting compliments and praise; usually because they feel embarrassed by the attention.

Accepting a compliment graciously though, tells the other person that you appreciate what they have to say about you. See accepting a compliment as a compliment in itself; that you trust and appreciate their judgement and opinion.

Focus on *receiving* the compliment rather than on its content. This helps you to acknowledge the compliment and express appreciation for it being given to you.

Imagine someone had given you a gift. How would you respond? Most likely, you would say 'Thank you'. Accept a compliment like a gift; just say 'thank you'. It's polite and gracious. If you want to add something, don't say 'it was nothing'. Anything else you add to 'Thank you' should be positive.

- 'How kind, thank you.'
- 'That's the best thing anyone has said to me today (this week/in a long time). Thanks!'
- 'Thank you for telling me.'
- 'Thank you. I really appreciate hearing that.'
- 'Thank you. I'm pleased too.'

when taking a compliment, smiling says a lot

If you do nothing else, smile. When taking a compliment, smiling says a lot without requiring you to say anything.

Share the credit. If you receive a compliment on a job well done and you didn't do it alone, make sure you acknowledge those who helped. 'Louise, Jane and Claire were a big help. I couldn't have done it without them.'

brilliant recap

- Giving compliments, appreciation and gratitude let the other person know that their actions have had a positive impact.

- Give a clear reason why you are complimenting or praising the other person. Acknowledge personal qualities or special efforts. Explain how their actions have made you feel.

- Know that for some people and in some cultures, it is polite to deny compliments.

- When it's appropriate, send a letter, card or email expressing your appreciation.

- If you find it difficult to accept compliments and praise, remind yourself that *accepting* a compliment is a compliment in itself.

- Accept a compliment like a gift; just say 'thank you' and smile.

CHAPTER 14

Procrastination and guilt

Did you decide to go for a run last week but kept putting it off? Do you have every intention to cut down the amount of hours you work and spend more time with family? Perhaps you keep promising yourself that you're going to finally make a date to meet up with old friends. Did you fail to keep your good intentions? Did you feel guilty about it?

Guilt's purpose isn't to make you feel bad just for the sake of it. Like so many other emotions, guilt is a helpful emotional warning sign; its purpose is to let you know when you've done something wrong. Guilt helps you to examine what you did or didn't do; you compare how you behaved with how you intended to or think you should have behaved. This knowledge alone can motivate you to change your behaviour. But too often, guilt creates stress and anxiety, which can make it harder to get back on track.

If you're in the habit of putting things off you've probably become very good at coming up with other activities that are, all of a sudden, more important or enjoyable.

It's easy to persuade yourself, for example, that going for a run can wait. Right now, cleaning the car or the kitchen is more important. Of course, under normal circumstances, cleaning the car or kitchen wouldn't be considered pleasurable activities, but compared with going for a run, a bit of cleaning becomes an attractive alternative!

Or maybe you've persuaded yourself that you'll cut back on the hours you work once you've completed this project that's so important right now. Perhaps you've convinced yourself that it would be easier to arrange that get together nearer to Christmas.

The problem is, these approaches are counterproductive. Bad enough that you keep putting off that run, meeting up with old friends or cutting down your work hours, but, as recent research shows, if you feel guilty about not having met your good intentions, you keep the bad feelings going and you'll find it even harder to motivate yourself the next time you attempt to fulfil your promises.[1]

You beat up on yourself as a way of getting motivated to do something. You 'should' do this, you 'must' do this, you 'ought' to do this, and so on. This doesn't make you want to do it, it only makes you feel guilty frustrated and resentful.

Guilt can drain your energy and divert your focus. And, because of the negative thoughts you have that are associated with whatever you didn't do, you will find it more difficult to do whatever you failed to do the first time round.

> guilt can drain your energy and divert your focus

This negative thinking sets up a cycle of failure and delay, as plans and goals are put off, pencilled into the diary for the following day or week again and again.

Of course, it's easy to believe that if you let yourself off too easily you'll just continue to put things off. But, the research shows that people who forgive themselves for their transgressions tend to do better on the next attempt than people who give themselves a hard time.

Accept how you feel

As with so many emotions, the best possible use of guilt is to experience it, acknowledge it, figure out what needs to be done, and move on.

Start by putting it into perspective. Rate your guilt. Out of ten, make two ratings. First, how bad the thing is that you've done, and second, how guilty you feel.

Note that guilt is a *feeling* that you have done wrong. It doesn't necessarily mean that you *have* done something wrong. So, try to figure out why you feel guilty – what, exactly do you think you've done wrong? Why do you feel guilty about it?

The next step is to experience, accept and take responsibility for what you did or didn't do and how you feel about it. So, no you *didn't* go for a run and you *haven't* cut down your work hours and yes, you *did* fail to contact your old friends. Accept that you're human – not a machine who will get on with things with a flick of a switch.

accept that you're human – not a machine

Learn from your mistakes

Although you can't change what you did or didn't do, you can learn from it. There's a number of possible reasons why you didn't meet your good intentions:

Feeling overwhelmed with the pressure. Putting things off can often be a way of coping with the anxiety you feel about the activity.

High expectations. Maybe you set your sights too high? Perhaps you have unrealistic ideas about what you're capable of or 'should' be doing. Expectations that are based on ideas of perfection can be difficult to achieve.

▶

You blame external circumstances. You tell yourself for example, that you were too tired for a run. Or, you need to work this much to pay the bills. Or, it's hard enough fitting your social life into your busy life, without squeezing old friends in too.

Whatever the reason for your procrastination, if your mind, your 'inner critic', reprimands you, you start to feel guilty and give yourself a hard time for failing to fulfil your intentions. You've set up negative ways of thinking that will only serve to drag you down further.

Once you've accepted your guilt and understood what went wrong, you need to make it less likely you'll put things off in future. Set yourself up for success; think positive! There are a number of ways you can do this:

- **Prepare yourself.** Be clear what your goals and expectations are and how they can fit into your life. If, for example, you simply want to get more fit, is there an easier way to build exercise into your week? What about simply going for a brisk walk each lunchtime?

- **Be more realistic.** Set achievable goals. Goals are in the future, but thinking about them is in the present. If thinking about what you need to do makes you feel good, it's realistic, *if not, if it makes you feel overwhelmed or stressed,* break it into smaller parts or change your goal. For example, rather than finish work at 5pm every day, start by finishing work at 5pm just one day a week.

- **Make it enjoyable.** If, for example, you really like walking, drop the run and find as many reasons as possible to walk everywhere.

- **Get support.** Identify the positive people in your life and tell them about your intentions. For example, contact the most proactive person in your group of friends and ask him or her to help you organise the reunion. Positive people will encourage you.

brilliant example

Marie has two children, aged two and six. She works four days a week as a PA. 'In the new year, I signed up for a marathon in June. I intended to train by going for a run each morning before work. On the Sunday night of the first week my two year old kept me awake half the night so I was too tired to go running in the morning. I was frustrated that the week had got off to a bad start. I managed to go on Tuesday but when I got to work, my manager said a deadline had been moved forward. This meant I would have to get up early the next morning and get to work – no time for a run.

By Thursday I was feeling *so* annoyed that I had only run once that week. I figured there was no point going on Friday – that's my day off from work. Instead, I told myself I'd start again next week. Monday came around and I actually forgot! I forgot to go for a run. I did manage to go the next day, but, then, I had an overnight trip so I missed another session. I didn't make it on the last two days of the week. This pattern kept up for the next month. I felt guilty that I was hardly ever going and considered pulling out of the marathon.

Talking it over with a friend, I realised I had unrealistic expectations. What was I thinking? Go running every day, work *and* look after a young family?

Instead of beating myself up about it, I decided to be more flexible. I would go for a run as and when I could fit it in. On the days I couldn't get there, I would go for a brisk walk at lunchtime instead. This positive approach made all the difference – I actually developed a pattern of going for a run three times a week.

brilliant recap

- Too often, guilt creates stress and anxiety, which can make it harder to get back on track.
- People who forgive themselves for their transgressions tend to do better next time around than people who berate themselves.

- The best use of guilt is to experience it, acknowledge it, figure out what needs to be done and move on.

- Put things into perspective. What, exactly do you *think* you've done wrong? Why do you feel guilty about it?

- Take responsibility for what you did or didn't do and learn from your mistakes.

- Make it less likely you'll put things off in future. Set yourself up for success; think positive!

CHAPTER 15

Give bad news

Apart from *receiving* bad news, one of the toughest emotional challenges is to *deliver* bad news.

If you need to deliver bad news, what matters most is how well you listen and respond to the other person.

Sometimes, the need to give bad news comes completely unexpectedly. If you need to give the news right away, say, 'I need to talk with you about...' This at least establishes a setting and a context for the conversation, instead of just blurting out the news.

Other times, you can prepare what you're going to say and anticipate the reaction and questions the other person might have.

First, know that you must lay it out plainly. Give basic information, simply and honestly. For example:

- 'Well kids, I'm afraid it's not good news. Disneyland is completely full. We won't be able to go this summer.'
- 'It's not good news – your funding bid was not successful.'
- 'I've got some bad news. Your laptop is beyond repair. I'm afraid I was unable to retrieve the first three chapters you'd written for your book.'

Start by listening, instead of talking

You may want to assess understanding first: what does the other person already knows or expect? Begin with a few open-ended questions: 'How old was your laptop? Have you had much trouble with it recently?' or 'How are you managing without your laptop since it stopped working?'

Imagine that the other person's reply was, 'I only bought it a year ago. That laptop's been nothing but trouble. I'm fed up with it and I've pretty much given up all hope with it.'

Your next response should reflect your understanding of how the other person feels. For example, 'So you've been pretty frustrated with it.'

When you deliver bad news to a person, you must deal with two issues: the facts *and* his or her emotional reaction to the bad news.

Be prepared for strong emotions. Acknowledge those emotions. Unless the bad news affects you directly too, try not to get emotional yourself.

You can't fix the laptop, change the funding decision or force the holiday company to provide a holiday. But you can acknowledge the other person's disappointment or anger: 'I'm sorry you're so upset. I can see this makes things difficult for you', or 'I can see this is disappointing for you.'

Do not say 'I know just how you feel', or 'Try not to worry about it.' Although you might mean well, the other person may well feel that actually, you *don't* understand or you're trying to move off the subject.

Anticipate questions and be prepared with answers and reasons

If you don't have the answers, say so. If you know where the other person can get information that might help to answer their questions, say so.

If a question is complicated, rephrase it to simplify it, but without changing the meaning. If it's angry, recast it in neutral language. Try to remain calm and answer those questions with respect and sensitivity.

For example, if the other person said 'Have you checked with Mandy who wrote the needs analysis? Did she provide the right information to the funders? She's bloody hopeless. What do the events team think about it? They're going to be really pissed off.' You could respond by replying 'Yes, the needs analysis that Mandy provided was complete and up to date. The events team haven't been told yet.'

Offer alternatives

Do you have any ideas or information that will help to resolve the situation? If so, offer to share it with the other person after you have listened to their response. State what, if anything, you can do to help, or ask 'Is there anything I can do?' Suggest possible actions, direction or ideas on what steps to take next. Focus on what can be done rather than what can't be done.

Say something positive. This is *not* to imply that things aren't that bad. The reason to include something positive is so that the other person has something positive to grasp. For example: 'But, you still have time to apply to another organisation for funding', and 'We *will* still have a holiday this summer.'

Should you always deliver bad news in person? It may seem easier to give bad news via email or letter for a couple of reasons. First, you can plan exactly what to say and how to word it and, second, you can also say what you want to without being interrupted. On the other hand, you can't see how the other person feels and responds. And if that's the reason for putting it in writing, you've taken the coward's way out!

When you deliver bad news in person, you can pick up clues from the other person's expressions and body language and emphasise, moderate or repeat what you've said accordingly. You can check understanding and clarify misunderstandings. So when you can, talk to the other person, face to face.

How to give bad news in writing

If you have to give bad news in writing be aware that just as the way that you deliver bad news in person can affect how it is received, the same is true when giving bad news in writing. The introduction is important. It gives you an opportunity to set the context for the bad news. Context (the circumstances relevant to the issue) can make a difference to how bad news is grasped and understood. For example:

Thank you for your funding application. This year we have had a three fold increase in applications, from a wide variety of community organisations. At the same time, the funds available to award to community groups has decreased by 20 per cent. We have reviewed your application and we have come to a decision.

the aim is not to delay the bad news, but to place it in context

The aim is not to delay the bad news, so much as it is to place it in context. You need to introduce it, and you need to give the bad news in context.

After you've set the context, state the bad news plainly and clearly.

Unfortunately, your application was not successful this time.

You will need to explain why.

Your project does not meet one of the five 'Communities Grants' outcomes.

Phrases and words to avoid

Being clear and direct doesn't mean you should be blunt and brutal in the words you choose or how you phrase the information. There is no guarantee that the reader won't be upset by your letter, but some words can be very unhelpful. For example, be cautious with words such as *clearly* or *obviously* – 'Obviously, not all bids would be successful' – because things might not be clear or obvious to your reader. Also, using words like 'obviously' and 'clearly' comes across as patronising.

Other words and phrases that should be avoided when delivering bad news include the following:

- You failed to
- You obviously did not
- You must accept
- You will never
- Impossible

Anticipate any questions the recipient might have, and answer them in the explanation.

This can then be followed by a suggestion for improvement or course of action.

You may want to apply for one of our other funding streams. You can speak to one of our advisors or visit our website for more details.

Bad news is one thing. Dwelling on it is what makes reading them bad. If you put the bad news in the proper context and, when possible, put it in terms as a difficulty that could be overcome then you leave the reader feeling hopeful and more positive, while being completely honest about the situation.

brilliant recap

- When you deliver bad news you must convey the facts *and* manage the other person's emotional reaction.

- Set the scene – find out what the other person already feels or knows. If you are giving bad news in writing, set the context first.

- Give basic information, simply and honestly.

- Listen to what the other person says in response to the bad news. Anticipate questions. Offer ideas or information that might help.

- Be positive. Focus on what can be done rather than what can't be done. Give the other person something positive to grasp.

Conclusion

A t whatever point in this book you started reading, you will have come across tips and exercises. Although I hope you've tried some of them out, don't feel that you've got to try out every single one.

Changing the way you think and behave takes time and practice. So, for example, in Chapter 7 I suggest that when you are asking someone about what they think and feel that you 'Make sure that you give him or her enough time to respond. They may need to think before they answer, so don't interpret a pause as an opportunity for you to take over the conversation.' If you usually jump in and break even the shortest of silences, you're going to find this habit hard enough to break without trying to put all the other ideas and tips in this book into practice at the same time!

So, start with an exercise, tip or idea that's appealing and doable and keep coming back to the book for more ideas when you're ready.

Like most personal development issues, there won't come a point where you can say, 'That's it, I've learnt and put into practice everything there is to know. I now have 100 per cent emotional intelligence.' But, if you use this book to take regular small steps, you'll soon improve your ability to identify and manage emotions in a range of situations. You'll have Brilliant Emotional Intelligence!

References

Chapter 1

1. Anderson, A. (2006) University of Toronto, 2006 Proceedings of the National Academy of Sciences.

Chapter 4

1. Parrott, W. Gerrod (2000) *Emotions in Social Psychology: Essential Readings (Key Readings in Social Psychology)*, 1st edn. Psychology Press, 23 Nov.

2. Plutchik, R. (1980) *Emotion: Theory, research, and experience: Vol. 1. Theories of emotion.* New York: Academic Press.

3. 'Culture moderates the self-regulation of shame and its effects on performance: The case of salespersons in the Netherlands and the Philippines'. *Journal of Applied Psychology* 88, Apr. 2003: 219–33.

Chapter 5

1. Galinsky, A., Huang, L., Gruenfeld, D. and Guillory, L. (2011) 'Powerful postures versus powerful roles: which is the proximate correlate of thought and behavior?', *Psychological Science* January 1, 2011 22: 95–102.

2. Carney, D., Cuddy, A. and Yapp, A. (2010) 'Power posing: brief nonverbal displays affect neuroendocrine levels and risk tolerance', *Psychological Science* October 2010, 21, 10: 1363–8.

Chapter 6

1. Sheppes, G., Scheibe, S. and Gross, J.J. (2011) 'Emotion-regulation choice', *Psychological Science*, 22, 1391–6.

Chapter 7

1. Neal, D.T. and Chartrand, T.L. (2011) 'Embodied emotion perception: amplifying and dampening facial feedback modulates emotion perception accuracy', *Social Psychological and Personality Science* November 2011, 2: 673–8.

2. Schachter, S. and Singer, J.E. (1962) 'Cognitive, social and physiological determinants of emotional state', P*sychological Review*, 69, 379–99.

Chapter 14

1. Wohl, M.J.A., Pychyl, T.A. and Bennett, S.H. (2010) 'I forgive myself, now I can study: How self-forgiveness for procrastinating can reduce future procrastination', *Personality and Individual Differences*, 48, 803–08.

Index